As the World Burns

Writers and Artists Reflect on a World Gone Mad

An Indie Blu(e) Publishing Anthology

As the World Burns

Writers and Artists Reflect on a World Gone Mad

An Indie Blu(e) Publishing Anthology

Indie Blu(e) Publishing
Havertown, Pennsylvania

As the World Burns: Writers and Artists Reflect on a
World Gone Mad
Copyright 2020 Indie Blu(e) Publishing

For information, address
Indie Blu(e) Publishing
indiebluecollective@gmail.com

ISBN: 978-1-951724-04-7 Paperback
          978-1-951724-05-4 EBook
Library of Congress Control Number: 2020949699

Editors:
Kindra M. Austin
Candice Louisa Daquin
Rachel Finch
Christine E. Ray

Cover Design:
Carrie L. Weis

Dedication

We dedicate this book to those who have bravely fought the encroaching darkness in 2020 with their writing and art, who have howled 'Black Lives Matter' and 'Not in my name,' and who insist that racism, sexism, homophobia, and war are not inevitable, or acceptable facets of the human condition. As the World Burns is a story of survival, and an act of resistance. We speak with many voices to the damage wrought in these violent, fevered months. Let us never forget or turn away from what is just, and what is necessary, to keep light alive in this world

Introduction

As Adrienne Rich once said, "If poetry is forced by the conditions in which it is created to speak of dread and of bitter, bitter conditions, by its very nature, poetry speaks to something different. That's why poetry can bring together those parts of us which exist in dread and those which have the surviving sense of a possible happiness, collectivity, community, a loss of isolation" (Moyers 1995, p. 342).

What does it mean to live through multiple, simultaneous pandemics?

The works in this volume take us on a journey through cities and towns, peeking in and out through windows and doors at our neighbors, at ourselves, as we navigate the precarity, uncertainty, frustration, grief, and the weight of the world since the start of the Covid-19 pandemic, the acceleration of climate change's devastating effects, increasingly visible police violence against Black and Brown communities and the resurgence of racism and antisemitism– not to mention a president who continues to fan the flames of division. The authors take us through their experiences, through the joy, laughter, sorrow, and fear. Some of them will bring a nod of recognition, reignite a spark of anger (or even more than a spark, maybe even a flame). The evocations of the loneliness and isolation weave through our losses– the loss of time, the loss of normalcy, the loss of flora and fauna, the loss of loved ones.

Some of the work in this volume riffs on "2020 vision" and "hindsight is 2020," as we ponder about what this year will bring us next. We work to navigate our fears, live through our isolation and our risk, wondering how long the world will be abnormal, wondering if this is the new normal. Trying to figure out how we survive, how we handle the pain of those who did not survive.

It also captures our anger at how much this year has heightened the challenges we already faced, but now loom so much larger. We are not blind to the ways that the transphobic, homophobic, xenophobic, anti-Semitic, racist element has both re-emerged in this pandemic and is heightened by the political divide, calling for a 'race war' by right-wing domestic terrorists, who shoot people in the streets while trying to lay claim to 'law enforcement.' The Covid pandemic has further weakened the bonds of community, and the isolation that we feel fan the flames of division and hatred while we try to keep ourselves, our loved ones, and that very community safe. Even before Covid, the constructed 'crisis' at the border reflects the ineptitude of the current administration and its cruelty, particularly its family separation policy that has left hundreds of children disconnected, perhaps permanently, from their parents.

The world burns, indeed, both figuratively and literally. Devastating fire seasons, in Australia and the US west coast. Areas within cities burn, after police respond violently to peaceful protesters (and right-wing terrorist groups keep trying to start that race war by starting fires). We choke in the smoke from fires, natural and man-made, struggling more and more to breathe. The refrain "I can't breathe" takes on added significance.

How do we connect with each other in these times? The works offered here provide us with a kind of connection; the mutuality of shared experiences that create community, even if that community is strained and often sad/anxious/afraid. As Rich's words remind us, poetry can be an essential balm in difficult times, reminding us that we are not alone in our sadness, our anxiety, our fear.

I am reminded of the importance of a forest fire's other function– to clear away the old, return nutrients to the soil, and to promote new growth. There is hope through the smoke and flames, like the morels that emerge the year after a forest fire. In my desert home, the sadness of the loss of forest is tempered by the understanding that new growth will emerge, and if conditions are right, the earth will bless us with the fire morels that are among the first signs of new life in the forest.

Like the fire morels, the final poems here offer us a brief vision of hope– that we can emerge not unscathed, but renewed in our connections with each other, and our care for the earth.

Lisa M. Anderson, PhD
October 25, 2020

Moyers, B. 1995. *The Language of Life*. New York: Doubleday.

Acknowledgements

Indie Blu(e) Publishing extends great thanks to our gifted cover artist, Carrie Weis, and all of the stellar *As the World Burns* contributors. We are truly honored that you entrusted us with your creative works.

Lisa Anderson, PhD, we thank you for your willingness to read *As the World Burns*, and to write a thoughtful and insightful introduction to the anthology.

Patricia Harris, and Chaitali, we thank you for your generous time spent reading *As the World Burns*, and for using your talents to write advanced reviews.

A special thank-you goes to the kind, and meticulous, Kristiana Reed. She is an invaluable friend of Indie Blu(e). Her continuous support of our projects is felt in all of the editor's hearts.

Peace, love, and light,
The Editors

Contents

Plague

Masks of the Red Deaths
Sean Heather McGraw

Listen my child to skeleton's last dance
Macabre though it may be, don't stand ajar
In lack of sympathy, we are not first
Nor last twill ever be who dances the jig
Of Fortune's drum and hears the fiddle's key.

When Bocaccio did write his famous book
The Decameron— ten stories of life
And death in Florence old, the fourteenth century
He knew the stress and fear we feel in Death's
Cold company. Lo, break the gate to hell
And let the sinners free, the plague we find

Is not aligned with who we want to be.
When Poe Master of Shadows fears all
Is lost for me, the Red Death claims all names
Will silent keep under the Masks we all
Now wear, will you weep for them who you know
And not give sympathy to those you don't?

The Plague has now made us on our bent knees
To whom do we pray? God of Eternal
Day, that must abide if we can fear subside
And deface our Red Pride to help our friends
Change Fortune's ends and wear the masks of Life.

Year of Doom (viewed from Europe)
Dawn D. McKenzie

As Australia was burning
Under a scorching sun
China's people started dying
In cold wintry Wuhan;

~

Soon, a pandemic was declared
Iran's Prime Minister
Was coughing his lungs 'On Air'
While Italian doctors were
Exhausted and crying in despair
Having to choose who got to breathe artificially
Who was going to live
And who didn't get assisted mechanically
And thus would die:
Between the 42 year old mother of three
Who had, for the past 2 years, been breast cancer free
And the 56 year old who had no children
But had never faced chemo or radiation?
And what about the 78 year old man?
How many added years to his life
Could a ventilator provide?
So many hideous questions
No doctor wants to have to face
In our so called civilized nations,
And as they fought with dignity and grace
Many carers suffered the ultimate sacrifice
To the unpreparedness of our countries' guides.

~

As the World Burns

At first, we could almost understand:
The virus was still unknown
China's numbers were mostly pretend
We only saw what they wanted shown
Propaganda.
But as Italy, France and Spain
Had more and more cases,
We started new knowledge to gain,
It all turned to races
Against the deadly strain
to stop the spread of the disease.

~

But still, no one would fancy
They too could suffer
What happened to Italy;
They obviously were so much better!
They'd forgotten maybe
The real problem was lack of money,
The unwillingness to prepare
For times with such a scare,
To have hospitals and stocks ready to go,
Rested nurses and doctors in constant flow
And, most importantly, a political team
Ready to take decisions, even extreme,
Hand in hand with the scientific society
Adapted as came each new discovery.
And so instead of frequent testing
And strict social distancing
To limit exposure and contamination,
Most countries had to resort to a lockdown.

~

Plague

The USA came later
But the virus struck from both borders.
You'd think that with Europe's precedents
And widely shared experience,
The fact we're all democracies,
All have similar economies,
They'd have heeded the warning,
As in a world with global living
News can travel as fast as viruses
And, looking at examples past,
Cooperating on licenses,
We could easily forecast
faster solutions for those coming last.
The US could have used
Valuable input, prepared better,
Taken some clues,
Followed Germany's lesson
Whose response was much softer
On the general population
And not as harsh on their economy.

~

Yet, it became clear early
That instead of looking at science, studies, experts and actual
facts,
People around the President
were more interested in political acts.
Instead of being about humanity
And how to prevent an exponential spread
It was all about someone's Twitter thread;
Pitching some states against others
In a fight to get much needed ventilators;

As the World Burns

Trying to outbid International allies
Out of airplane-full of medical supplies,
For Europe all ready to take off
Trying to bring them to LA; what a falloff
For a country that, if not revered
At least was once respected
By other democracies
Or self declared 'great economies'.

~

And it didn't stop there
Every day came a new nightmare;
The President supported
Non science-based conspiracies,
At the same time as he thwarted
Local governments policies
Urging for social distancing
The basics of mask-wearing.
He who wanted to make America great
Did it along the worst possible trait:
What was once the greatest nation on Earth
Is now the hotspot for Covid-19 disease.
Aside from a few billionaires
Who managed to get richer
The everyday American
Is struggling even more
No jobs available for the working poor
Thus healthcare goes and
Soon so do school and home.

~

As for International standing,
The White House refused to take part in discussions

Plague

With leaders of other countries and organisations
To find sources of financing
To unite
In the fight
Of the worldwide enemy
The USA could have shown leadership
But gave up their once hated or coveted grip
On the world.

~

For the first time in almost 8 decades
Europeans feel not much more than pity
For a Giant who once forced them into its shade
But now acts small and petty.

The Old Vic (world closed after Covid)
Johann Morton, Morton Labs

Unbuoyant
Kai Coggin

When there are no more tears for the dying,
where does all of that salt go?

Does it melt back
into the bodies of all who are left?

Do we swallow down an ocean
for her, and her, and him,
and brother, papa, auntie, love?

Do we become more buoyant in
our numbness?

How do we memorialize the names of 85,000
strangers? Even just to say all of their names
out-loud in a stream
would take days upon days.

Can you imagine how long their lives
would be strung end to end like that,
like those paper dolls that hold hands
unraveled, all their names,
one after another
like a sentence—
not a death sentence
but one that reads like a dream,
like a poem of everything beautiful
they ever conceived,
or a string of all their 85,000 smiles
and how it would stretch and reach out for miles, or
let's line up every time they smelled something
cooking and it warmed them up inside,

As the World Burns

or a poem of all of their dancing and
romancing and enchanting the fate of all
their fallen stars to give them a little
longer on earth
than the 85,000 numbers that they are.

They died alone.
That's the part that guts me.
Most of them died alone
while their families were locked down
not around, visitors are not allowed
to be there to hold their hands,
hand
to
hand
to
hand
unraveled,
separated isolated obfuscated
no one should have to die like that,
fill up freezer trucks with their cut short lives like
that, stack up black body bags to the sky like
that.

Yet here in America the numbers
still rise while states reopen to
capitalize
because the American Dream is there for the
chasing and there is no quarantine strong
enough
to stop this erasing
of lives
because half of us wear masks and
stay home and half of us (them) think
it's all just a lie.

Plague

Round and round this plague will flow,
where it stops,
nobody knows,

but mark this day for all of the dead
and mark tomorrow
and tomorrow
and tomorrow after that.

When there are no more tears for the
dying, where does all of that salt
go?

Does it melt back
into the bodies of all who are left?

Do we swallow down an ocean
for her, and her, and him,
and brother, papa, auntie, love?

Do we become more buoyant in
our numbness?
Because today I sit at a table
of salt, I turn back to their
names
and become a pillar of
salt, I open my
hands
and search for paper dolls
fallen stars
something
someone
to reach back.

Times that Try
F.I. Goldhaber

These times try our souls in the court of adversity
as a global pandemic reveals our true natures.

Some reached out, helped where they could: providing free
lunch
to students who only eat at school; running errands
for home-bound, frightened seniors; donating needed funds,
supplies, masks; offering amusements, delivery.

Buying gift cards and meals to donate and deliver
to health care workers, helping struggling restaurants
while thanking those risking their lives serving every day.

But, scammers, hackers, bankers, politicians only
saw an opportunity for profit. Dumping stock;
gouging prices; forcing employees to risk their health;
sacrificing a thousand lives for a market bump.

Taking advice from Wall Street instead of doctors and
scientists; refusing to lock down and prevent the
viral spread; delaying tests in search of more profits;
denying sick leave, health care; bailing out megacorps.

Partying on the beach rather than forgo spring break
festivities; gathering at clubs and restaurants;
choosing to endanger the old and vulnerable,
unwilling to make sacrifices for common good.

Plague

Demanding at-risk employees return to work in
hospitals; abandoning the innocent in care
facilities; ignoring risks to immigrants in
concentration camps, POC in profit prisons.

Maliciously pushing harmful snake oil, defective
supplies; stealing tips from those who deliver; coughing
on bus drivers; licking groceries, parcels, door knobs.

Ammosexuals gathering on state capitol
steps—armed with automatic weapons, racism, white
supremacy—threatening those trying to protect
the lives of everyone except the imprisoned.

The trial of souls in the court of adversity and
so many failed to exhibit basic compassion.

Arrival of Spring
Annette Kalandros

Spring arrived
Barely seen.
Our eyes turned inward.
Suspicious of air,
We could not take spring
Deeply into our lungs,
Feel the warmth of it on our skin,
Taste the freshness of it on our tongues
For fear.

We counted our first born
And tried prayer.
Had we forgotten the blood of the lamb
Above the lintel?

We sought protection in distance,
longing for human touch.
Hate and fear drained us.
We grew weary hearing–
Wash your hands
Don't touch your face
Wash your hands
Prayed Mother Mary full of grace
Six to ten feet apart we must stand
We feared to touch

Plague

Our mothers
Our fathers
Our sisters
Our brothers
Our sons
Our daughters
And longed–
All the more–
For touch.
Yes, this will make us aware—
Appreciate what now
We could not do.
Yes, we would improve,
We would appreciate all.
Technology would see us through.

Somewhere in our collective soul
We had doubts, questions–
We had to know–
Hadn't there been signs?
HIV, Ebola, Bird flu, Swine flu,
Zika, West Nile too,
All killers, all unseen—
Hurricanes, droughts,
Famines, earthquakes—
Natural disasters ripping
The world to shreds.
Had we done this to ourselves?

We hadn't been the good stewards
We were charged to be.
Drowning seas with plastic, killing bees,

16

As the World Burns

Melting ice caps, making greenhouse gases–
Killing the mother God gave us.
We hadn't loved each other as we were loved,
As we were instructed to do.
Then our arrogance, a weed within our souls grew.
We killed, pillaged, maimed, raped, started wars–
For the one skin that made us master,
For the name of God, the only one to worship,
For riches, since the strong should prey upon the weak,
For gender, after all women were things to use,
For sexuality, holy books said there's but one way to love,
For everything was ours to take.

We'd killed each other
For these grotesquely grandiose ideas,
While calling ourselves godly,
Saying our actions were sanctioned
By our God, our religion.
Only we knew the natural order of things.
In pride, we claimed
Where we walked—
Holy Ground.
Then guilt filled our lungs,
We finally questioned—
Was this it–
The fourth seal broken?
Had the pale rider been loosed
Upon the land?
While wanting to believe
It was all simply science.

confirmed coronavirus cases in baltimore county at 10,924
dani bowes

my sister is now part of a data set
receiving back to back calls from the health department
trying to weave a web of her connections
from the past two weeks.
as her head pounds like her feet on the pavement
chasing after me at five years old,
trying to teach me how to ride my bike,
they prod about her hygiene
like she wasn't the skeleton of a hospital
an essential worker
reminding everyone to wear a mask
wash their hands
stay six feet apart.
to researchers she is another case to be studied,
but to our family she is a sailor
instructing us how to unknot the binding ties
that kept us apart
the weight of disunion square on her shoulder blades
as we cawed and clawed at one another.
as a nurse tickles my brain with q-tips
i think of how we voyeuristically watched wuhan
implode into themselves -
whispering it's the other, not us, not amerikkka
while my sister clings to her bedsheets
repeating that this is not another nightmare.

What Are Your Rights, Really?
Tremaine L. Loadholt

If you don't live in a
constant state of "I hope
I can get through two weeks
without contact from a
patient who tested positive
for this damn virus" as your
normal, then I don't want to
hear
about your rights.

I am a person who spends
more time surveying adults
while wolfed in PPE, in front
of an unsecured station,
armed with a trusty
thermometer. You want to
bitch & moan about a state's
reasons to
scale back on reopening,
you can't lean on these
shoulders. No, I won't lend you
an ear.

I crave some semblance
of normalcy just like you,
but I'm doing my part.
I want to see a flattened
curve, children running
around
without their faces

Plague

covered, & wrap my family
in an
enveloping embrace.

But, I'm stuck in this
hamster-wheel with
squealing people who'd
rather risk rising numbers in
cases and deaths than put
on a mask.
The bulk of my day
includes batting down
the eager
who've spent several days
out in public rather
than isolated at home.

My mind is a spinning
top, endless spinning—
yet you bark about not
being able to be free.
Free from
what exactly? You
wouldn't know freedom if it
laid
up with you and got
you pregnant.
You are selfless, senseless,
and stubborn.

Now tell me, what are
your rights, really?

Everyone is a Fucking Expert
Philip A. Wardlow

People become afflicted
become sickened
A Mother dies, a Father dies
a Brother, a Sister,
a Nephew, an Aunt,
that crazy fun Uncle,
well he's no longer around.
Yet some know better,
some are fucking experts on everything now:
Epidemiology, Politics
and the Constitution, here
come take your diploma
young ignorant man.
They have just crawled from
the primordial ooze,
but without an ounce of knowledge or true
reflection,
they know the why, the what, and the wherefore
of it all.
Without doubt or reservation,
they string together tens of hundreds
of stories into
a conspiracy of disdain and ridiculousness.
Anxiety now rules an already twisted logic system,
mutating them all into something
new and improved,
The truest most deadly virus of
a thing called the Fool.

Droplets
Rachel Kobin

Droplets
Rachel Kobin

What frightened
the medical student,
more than any blood or gore?
water, water, gushing out.

What frightens the doctor most?
don't drink bleach, but
don't drink the water, water gushing in
thousands of droplets.

Don't drink bleach
if you want to live,
keep the droplets in
keep the virus out.

If you want to live,
turn the finger of blame around,
the virus, not Gina, not testing
His lies kill.

Turn the blame where it lies
and frightens most.
His lies murder
more than any blood or gore.

Pandemonium
Marcia Weber

it started with a little bug
a lightening tug
smuggled in a hug
    and all the world now
huddles afraid

        souls seek solace
        suffering soothed
        sodden in the sniffling
        storm

mouths in mulish moues
marinating in malicious
mucus of myriad
moaning municipalities

        cells rust with *drip*
        monochrome clip
        insidious grippe
        of metallic coughs

silent screams
crusted onomatopoeia
of rented
tented
lives

As the World Burns

slaver of demons
purports to cool
toasted brows
shards of fear
lodge in my throat

yet I breathe

and in the numinous sunlight
the mourning dove coos

No superheroes
Melita White

The days now pass without much to define
All hope of progress halts, is now in doubt
When will it cease, this endless pause of time?
The stagnant wait is now what life's about
We don our masks and faces disappear
No superheroes in this viral world
Fine particles are airborne, cause just fear
And added risk all wits will come unfurled
Hostilities and protests emanate
In city streets and on the internet
Tense waves of pain and tension escalate
Debates are full of ugly epithets
For humans to survive this dreaded scourge
We must unite or greater be the purge

Falls the Shadow
John W. Leys

How does the world end?
With incompetence and greed,
Snuffed out by an
Apocalyptic plague
Because inconvenience outweighs
Individual lives.
Because economics outweigh
The Angel of Death.
As billionaires and politicians
Gladly grind your bones
To dust
In the gears and cogs
Of the capitalist machine.

Wall Street
Sarah Ito

Too Much Pork: Day 31 of the Quarantine
Henri Bensussen

TV airs the news: too many pigs. Meat plants
shut down, workers infected by the Virus
unable to transform squealers to neat packages
of pork as they pile up in pens, piglets aging
into porkers, no space at the farm for this overflow.
Camera pans to eyes like ours, full of questions—
What's happening to us?

Do they know how their world is turning
wrong side out? No tackle ties them to threader
racked up and pulled through the slasher.
Farmers talk euthanasia, pigs look stunned,
they feel what's coming, a new way to die
they'll have to adapt to and accept, to keep
the farmer going, who can't give them away.

If only we could imagine it, that thru the magic
of algorithms pork could be funneled to the hungry
rather than buried in a field. A forfeiture of life
to give life: instead it's withholding:
a wasteland in our land of plenty.

Plague

3/29/20
A. Lawler

The world snapped its fingers
And I went home to rest.
Opened the balcony door
Let the clean air in.
Curled up in bed
With a book
And read in that lovely grey light.
All the children are home from school.
We have been told to sit on the stairs and think about what we
have done.
The city is quiet
A husband with his back turned in bed
The room is still.
My love has not forgiven me yet.

Postcard from Pandemic
Robert Okaji

They stack their cart with essentials:
frozen garlic, six packages of grilled
mushrooms, fifteen cans of garbanzo
beans, three bottles of truffle oil and
enough alkaline water to float a fleet
of dinghies. There is, alas, no hand
sanitizer, no toilet paper. You must
decide, he says, between the jar of
organic marinara and the 2% milk.
Weighing need against desire she
chooses the sauce, then selects a
bundle of the brightest daffodils.

"Postcard from Pandemic" was originally published in *Vox Populi*,
March 2020.

Bananas
Irma Do

I sit on my overstuffed couch
Scrolling on my iPhone
Waiting
Impatiently for groceries
Annoyed
At not being able to get all the food
I ordered from that same couch
Two weeks ago

She sits in her secondhand Honda
Giving her phone to her toddler
Popping the trunk
Opening her door in the rain
Gathering two bags at a time
Making five trips
Leaving them on the covered porch
After ringing the doorbell
And then swiftly getting back into her car

I open the door
Dismayed that two bags had fallen over
And the cereal had gotten wet
I see her drive off with the toddler in the back
Eating a banana
And I wonder if that's why I didn't get bananas in my groceries.

Digital artifacts from March 2020
Kendall Krantz

1. **Act I: Tinder or text messages (good luck figuring out which)**

Ethan: ik know ur my RA but lets spend one last night together before getting evicted XP it'll b fun i promise bc im not a virgin and basically not a freshman anymore either

Tania: I think you're the girl my boyfriend cheated on me with while I was traveling … you may want to get an STD test. Crazy to see you on here! You're cute, I can see why he liked you so much. Let's grab coffee some time, maybe next fall?

Mary: Hey, if you're home could you come babysit?

Ethan: come onnnnnnn

Rachel: Do you have the stats homework?????

Mom: So excited you're home! Come down for dinner!!!!!!!111!!

Dongju: hey cutie :) wanna hang?

Jeff: Can't believe you're home! Wanna smoke in the park where we went in high school? Lol

Summer: Back to Atlanta? Wanna get down to business again???? ;)

Ethan: shoulda done it u missed out

Plague

Mom: Can you put the clean clothes in the dryer? Luv u

Dongju: sry I kissed u then it was wrong im sorry

Summer: shrooms are half off. Today only!!!!!

Mary: 8:00pm tonight pls. $75. wear a mask.

Dongju: hey what's up sorry I was drunk. wanna hang?

Rachel: I think I failed stats.

Dongju: Did you make it home safe? You seemed pretty gone last night.

Mom: Sleeping so late! R u dead? Lol let's go for a hike.

Summer: restocked on Mary Jannnnneee

Rachel: Should I take next year off?

Dongju: Hey, everything that's going on seems like a lot. LMK if there's anything I can do to help or if you just wanna chill quietly. We don't have to do anything. I'll make you dinner or smthn. If you're not into me that's fine. We can just be friends. I'd just feel bad leaving you alone right now.

Mom: Dad flew out to see Papa. Call him to support please.

Ethan: Hi whens registration for next semester can u help me pick a CS class sry

Tania: So it turns out Raj is clean dw about it :) sry if that caused any confusion ik clinics are closed. Oops!

Ethan: hi

Dongju: Just come over to change the environment. You'll feel better, I promise.

Mary: Can u do tuesday 2p?

Rachel: can we ft?

Mom: Call Dad.

Dongju: You okay?

Ethan: hi

2. **Act II: Google searches from roughly the same time**
Brown University COVID-19 response
Is flying safe?
How to fly safely
Under 24 hour movers
Tickets to Atlanta
Delta one way ticket to Atlanta
Spirit airlines one way ticket to Atlanta
Pandemic babysitting safety measures
Sugar daddies Atlanta
Being sober at your parent's house
~~Wine shop~~
What does herpes feel like?

Plague

Open STD clinics near me
Open STD clinics near me free
Open STD clinics near me free socially distant
Thai takeaway
Home testing for herpes
Explaining a pandemic to seven y/o
Cancer survival rate
Cancer survival rate grandpa age
How to go through a 12-step plan from home
~~Wine shop~~
How to cope with an STD diagnosis
Remote jobs for college students
Remote AA
Rehab Zoom
Palliative care Cleveland
Online casket delivery
Zoom Minyan
Zoom Kaddish
Wine shop

Before COVID We Had Curtains
Jamie L. Smith

The blonde
in the unbuttoned red blouse

sits at a mission style desk
in the house next door,

watches me—naked,
I drop to my knees

 by the bedside
—12:14am—fishing

between infant dust bunnies
and unopened books

on mindfulness
for a faint spark

from the latest dropped earring.
Her son is asleep, lights out

since 11:23. She rises—12:16—
sashays

her soundless merengue
rubbing plates dry in her kitchen,

Plague

hot-pink dishcloth
tossed over her shoulder,

hips shimmying back
and forth.

All Thumbs
Maria Gianna Iannucci

She has been twiddling everything but her thumbs in social isolation. In need of ventilation, she cracks the window back and undoes the front snap letting fruit fall in season. A man on the street is the only one who sees them and bows his head knowin', he ain't gettin' none as a newspaper scrapes pigeon droppings on its way to the subway station. She runs a hand over the small of her back, a little indentation above the vulnerable crack as she thinks about the night in Lido, the disco, and a bottle of Sangria, and wonders how the man on the bus in Rome got his hand under her skirt so fast. Horns from below show that the traffic is backed as she closes the sash knowing that the best company she has, is her own.

California Covid Sun
Marisela Brazfield

following the gray marbled filigree of last month's mud on
sidewalk downtown farmers market hot with California Covid
sun

the cherries look tempting but the purple Peruvian potatoes go
great with olive oil pink salt and cumin my face tightly masked
chewing the fat with the book vendors afoot offering their home
address for their monthly 'hope we get laid' poetry reading
salon

then the urban crows catch my eyes they with E A Poe smiles
rainbow oil slick feathers shine under that California Covid sun

Dr. TL tongue tab flash back dream hits me like a polar breeze
suddenly there is baby Grady golden brown moppy hair blue
Keds size three and an uncle with soldier rough hands smiling
at me

no sooner than a tear peeks into my water line a sonic whistle
from Spring Street punctures my loser mind Lola Ramirez on
the weekends and Manny Sandoval during the MF 9 to 5 she a
purple paisley mu mu gold earrings and Michael Kors sack me
black t shirt with the face of Siouxsie Sioux paper Trader Joe's
bag both aging X'ers under that California Covid sun

As the World Burns

Lola and i float to the flower stand and her throat crooned in a Yucatanian Spanish slang enchanting and schmoozing the vendors so i get to pay ten bucks for a 50 dollar assorted calla lily bunch

the 4 am 3 cup Turkish coffee buzz wore off and dull knife pain from old injuries descend upon my left arm so i shared a dream that a cool boy once had while Lolita and me sipped iced black pressed molassesed coffee under that California Covid sun

Untitled
Jimmi Campkin

Forward
Aakriti Kuntal

Morning's drool
trickles between thick palms,
nets of belonging stir.

The whistling gets louder.
It burns in the ear,
the flexing mold of skin.

Tick-tock: the eye of the clock
is the oblong bird that screeches
at night,

pecking at this somatic lump called
life. *Lauki*, *chapati*, masks, and pills.
Doctors on Practo,
and the stiff broil of ripe summer.

The body is baked in the heat
of its thoughts, the "ifs" and the "shoulds",

The starched tents of homeless men,
their scavenger shirts under the oval sun,
the dropping birds,
the large debate of life and morality
on Twitter,
the injustice, the arguments,
the compass that spins it all.

Baked breads fly on Instagram,
and strange insects

43

Plague

draw their dances on the sliding door

The white film of day slips
into my mouth,
silken tofu, florets and throat sores,

Thread by thread,
they make their way into the sleeping
gorge.

I imagine I'm at the white door of life.
Nothing passes here.
There is not the sound of a single speck.

My hands are dark purple
from carrying life,
clots of rinsed blood.

My hands are dark purple,
they have been for a while,
the body just gets richer.

My hands are dark purple,
popping pills and vowels,
every morning, waking and rushing,
trying again beneath a tap of water,

because sometimes just breathing again
is moving on.

*P.S.: Chapati: Indian bread, Lauki: Hindi word for the vegetable
Bottle Gourd*

Ticking
Sarah Bigham

The loud ticking of clocks clops my brain and itches my ears as I wait for the flares to subside. So I bought clocks with continuously swooping minute hands. They emit no annoying sounds, yet the arms never, ever stop – engaged in an endless game of chase they show me, perhaps even more clearly, how the passage of time never ceases, never slows. There is no fraction-of-a-second gap between moments. Time is running away, or at least looping constantly on a track, like my pet gerbils who used to run on their play wheels, never getting anywhere, but doing so industriously.

Essential
Milly Webster

"Nothing has really happened until it has been described."
   – Virginia Woolf

Press fast forward
to rewind
the trauma leftovers
of this year.

We have had to become comfortable
with the uncomfortable

In a moment of crisis, you must write
the 3-dimensional
becomes only an allusion
in a million different localities.

As the World Burns

5/30/20
A. Lawler

I have lost a summer that I have not seen yet.
Your husband stands in a swimming pool.
The sun is too bright.
It wakes me up at six a.m.
The pool is drained.
And we have lost a summer that we have not seen yet.

An Alchemy of Ingredients
Aakriti Kuntal

Velvet blue sleeps on the couch,
the shredding haze of mattress glistening
in the blue light of phones.

The body is the cream white walls.
It has the stench of ceramic
and the loneliness of air.

It is stiff as the cotton that infests
the furniture and moist as the molds
that decorate the bathroom walls.

The chores chew the day, and yet
in them a newfound companionship.

The kitchen is a garland.
Garlic leaks into the memories.
Peas swim in the flickering girth of water,

and the ladle is a song that slowly bangs and stirs.
Tiny moths of flour ride into the chimney sunset
and between arguments

and laughter, cooking is loving one another.
The balcony plants
are again the cynosure of all eyes, and tiny

As the World Burns

sparrows are extended children.
I wake to glazed, blue clouds
and the wafting dreaminess of cheese

mixes with the peculiar freshness of air
and coriander. The body forgets to retire
and the bp machine lays forgotten in a corner,

yet the pulse of the body is measured without a miss,
every day, against the flapping oboe
of the early bird's song.

I Want to Fly
Charu Sharma

We break against the dirt of the ground
with the loudest thud,
it's there for everyone to hear
it's there for everyone to see.
A glass pane put back together
from its broken shards
isn't as transparent;
you can trace the deep grayish sadness
running along the long lines of its cracks,
just on the brink of turning entirely opaque.

Under my navel
runs a deep chasm,
my voice has always gotten lost
in its depth;
the door to my room left slightly ajar
just to remind me
that there is a way out
from this all-consuming Dark.

This place is whimsical,
sometimes I am asphyxiated
while at others, I somehow catch a
whiff of breath.
Monotony in the constant murmurs,
a sign of commotion
yet it feels so soulless;
I am surrounded mostly by blinds,

As the World Burns

strictly confined in their designated
row number on a particular column,
while I am always spilling out
of this rigid structure,
wondering at the possibility
of an absolute silence:
Would it feel as much dead, or
could it deaden anymore?

A grey bird atop a penthouse
against the pinkish hues of the sky,
some purple splurted here
some orange intervened from there,
I overlooked
this one day
from a window running from floor to ceiling;
what an overwhelming quiet, what an absolute forgetfulness
that I didn't even realize that
at just that moment
I had developed an urge to fly!

Laying to Rest
Ali Grimshaw

I thought I was listening, while sun shone
through your voice and across the distant fields

where blocks of green in different shades lay still
while cars passed us by to follow each other down the road.

Your story of yesterday's sadness floated toward me gravel
crunching with our paired steps

the train of cars roadside, a singular person inside each.
"Maybe we shouldn't speak as we pass by," you said.

I do not know who The Pioneer Cemetery was welcoming or
how many were saying farewell, a silent awkward number

attended, while someone filled the hole with dirt, there were no
voices there to speak, only silent eyes through windows, birds
in the sky.

Someone was coming home to rest, where a last view down
the valley hushed us all.

Days later, I kept thinking about the people in separate cars
unable to hold each other in this disconnected time of grief

on a day in Spring when they needed to touch one another
during this time of goodbye, not meant for separation.

First shared on Visual Verse: An Anthology of Art and Words VOL. 07 Chapter 09.

In the Days of Silent Streets
Deirdre Fagan

We thought the world had closed,
as shops put up their "Be Back Soon" signs,
we waited each day for the news to bring
how long, how long.

Each house held one or more, at least two eyes
peering out at the abandoned pavement,
sparkling gravel, shuttered windows,
now much clearer skies.

While we took deep breaths inside, the earth exhaled
a deep sigh, a full chest inhale and exhale,
birds sang tree to tree in harmony,
the world opened to spring.

Pollution eased as we limited our bustling,
hustling—we slipped on looser pants, children
giggled up games, we created our own meals and
played the old way of telephone—yet many were dying.

We had once by choice ceased hearing voices,
exchanged dipthong for type, now only the
memory of chatter in the streets to compete
with bird's song, to reverberate with our own
hearts' beat.

Plague

Animals in captivity mated and the skies cleared for
all—but us. Holding tightly to this whirling ball,
I whispered, "The world has not yet closed,"
in your ear, or across the miles, "I am here,
I am here, I am here."

I-soul-ation
Dr. Sneha Rooh

This year, 2020, gave me the opportunity to do what I wanted to do and said I would do, with all good intention for so long- taking time to listen to myself without guilt. This is not the story of an overworked corporate tycoon, in my case a successful doctor who has forgotten to live her life.

In fact, three years ago, I packed my bags, gave up my job to travel across India to train people in Palliative care. I had asked life to live me and it did. I visited places, I never planned to visit and met people I wouldn't have otherwise met. I had patients from rural Kashmir come see me, gave lectures to monks from Nepal in Palliative care and ended up in Sweden to represent my work and in the Netherlands to attend a summer school- so you see, it's not that story. Despite doing all these things, despite being away from my 9 to 5 job, there was this sense of guilt and an inner rush- that guilt is what I had wanted to take a break from.

It's an irony that it was only when the whole world stopped, did I allow myself to. So much for all the rebellion and standing out! It was as if I needed people to go into the I-soul-ation with, and together we were. I joined the New York Writers Coalition writing workshop days before lockdown was announced in India. I heard the fears and shared mine. I attended webinars to see familiar faces and joined events to keep hearing human voices and I waited for touch.

Plague

Somewhere along the way, I started sleeping in and cooking for myself. I started having conversations over the phone without an agenda and being okay with it. I started posting my old family photos on Facebook and writing about them and my thoughts on them. Somewhere among the many webinars, I started choosing the ones I had long tip-toed around - the dream of learning about the healing capacities present within the body when we fully occupy it. It started with free summits and then to applying for scholarship courses, and then paying a subsidised fee to get enrolled into an arts-based therapy post graduate program. It has been an I-soul-ation for me. In fact, I think the whole spectrum from making dalgona coffees to submitting manuscript to publishing houses is the effect of I-soul-ation.

It has also pushed us to face what we had been running away from, that conversation with our spouse, the unspoken resentment with our parents, that discomfort at work, with nowhere "out" to go, we went in, a little if not fully. We also realised the freedom that came after. In fact, I think it was because of the Pandemic, the time it gave for us to touch our lives and souls, that George Floyd's murder didn't warrant the customary "Ah sad! One needs to be weary of rubbing the cops the wrong way" or "few are bad and few are good - what time is it again? I'm late for work". We have started seeing clearly what was always there and hearing clearly what we didn't hear before because of the fear and noise of the next place to reach, physically or in life.

As the World Burns

Now, like in the classic hero's journey, we have separated from our usual environment, we have been initiated into a different reality with the possibility of cleaner air, more time for learning from this slowing down. What will 'return' look like? What will a life filled with wisdom drawn from this time look like?

I would like to think that we will hug people longer, be grateful to be able to work, that we will smile brighter when the masks come off and we'll let the smiles fully enter our hearts, that we will be careful about the lies sold to us and remember that we are precious mortals with precious lives and an immense ability to connect and care.

Smiling with Your Eyes
Kai Coggin

There are over a million cases now,
I don't even have to name it
anymore, how it has spread
into all
of our poems like a contagion
and we don't know who
among us is carrying this ungodly crown,
when we walk the once space spaces of
our town, when we socially distance our
grocery trips, all flowing down in one
direction
like little frightened ships,

but no man is born to be an island,
and I am aching to make contact,

six feet away,
six feet away,
please stand six feet away
or you'll be six feet under in a grave,

what an interesting paradox,
but this time has so many of those—

doing NOTHING to save another
like the president,

As the World Burns

doing nothing to SAVE another
like all of us shuttered in our homes,

sheltered in place
our six degrees of separation
hold much more meaning now.

And what about meaning—
hasn't *everything* changed?
hasn't our whole paradigm shifted?
everything that we know,
all of our definitions are twisted and
turned in this new dimension of
unknown.

We casually tell complete strangers to *stay safe*
We begin e-mails with
I hope you and your family are healthy.

We watch as the unfathomable numbers grow
and grow. There is nowhere to put our dead.

Doesn't that old world we long for
seem like a distant memory
that's lost its tangibility?

Look how now we cringe
when we see commercials
of people in crowds all carefree
with their breaths and their hands
and their laughter!

Plague

Look at our hearts race
when we see old group pictures,
(God I miss group pictures)
squeezing into tiny frames,
no I can't see your head,
get in tighter,
get closer,
squeeze
say cheese! CHEESE!

But that was then
in the old world
pre-quarantine
47 days ago for me,
or is it 87,
or is it time to eat again?
and what day is it?
week?
month?
it's May?

2020 vision is wearing fear-colored
glasses and seeing the world
through tears.

All the whiskey is gone,
and no this is not easy for anyone,
and we all wear our collective grief in different ways,
in different shades of collective grey,

As the World Burns

and it is going to be a long time until all of this
goes away. So for today—
I go to the grocery store for supplies
wear my mask like a good citizen,
hold my hand sanitizer
like a lump of salvation in my pocket,
move through the produce section
the way that a magnet repels another
magnet, regret touching a
cantaloupe
to see if it is ripe,
the hyper-cognition of touch
of space
of whatever you do
don't touch your face!

I find myself
talking to myself
as I move through the store,
like whispering into a seashell
and hearing the ocean talk back,
my own mumbling,
in a sea of would-be bank robbers,
half-faced strangers,
silent shoppers.

I am a smiler and a small-talker,
I am a hugger and a handshaker,
none of which matter in this world,
and all that is left uncovered

Plague

above my mask
are my eyes,
and if eyes are windows to the soul,
then let mine be all the way open.

This morning in the mirror,
I practiced smiling
with my eyes,
put my hand over my mouth
and smiled with just the top half of my face
visible in the reflection,
and I admit it takes practice
to not look like you are just
shocked or your eyebrows
itch
or you're curious
and maybe smiling with your eyes
means just stopping and looking
deeper, holding a stare
where there once was a hand,
looking deep into another's window
when the smile is muted behind mask,

in this time of disconnection and
pan(dem)ic, it's one little thing I am
going to consciously do, look at people
in the eyes
until they feel my smile coming through.

sheltering in place w/Baudelaire
Rob Plath

 i read yr poem
"one o'clock in the morning"
10 X times today, baudelaire
i keep thinking of yr
self-imposed isolation
barricaded in yr tiny room
a mad lonely vampire
feeding from yr own
trembling wrists
writing w/ a bloody fang
thru the night
it's 1 am here
24/7, baudelaire
it's very strange
the front door
is a sad, mute rectangle
like a vertical grave
nobody walks thru
my society consists of:
my cat
& my typewriter
& bottles of pills
& something to wash
them down
past the eternal lump
in my throat
i poke the keys
of the machine

Plague

as the cat's question mark tail
floats past my stubbled jaw
my hair is growing
in this solitude
maybe i'll dye it green
like you once did, baudelaire
green as the grass
over graves
green strands glowing
in a bath of night
but for now i blend in
w/the darkness

Whitby
Jimmi Campkin

Emptying
Susi Bocks

the anger
is palpable
holding back
a muffled urge
steeliness
at the back
of the throat

trump
covid
deaths
agony
isolation
loneliness
restrictions
desperation
affected livelihoods
cashflow problems
emotional upheaval
life-altering change to our world

Self-Isolation
Jaya Avendel

I am hot and angry
Lost somewhere between crying and screaming.

I seek something to break
To fling a jar hard and
Watch its crystalline shine shatter
With this exile as I
Slowly dissolve into a pile of bones
Cracked without hope.

I thought myself strong and so
I am as my will keeps me here
Nerves breaking with each passing glance at the freedom
Rippling in the foam on the river.

In a broken mirror I see myself
Until the fragments merge and my soul flies wild strong.

I Think the Birds Don't Care
Kelsey Hontz

I resent the sun for shining.
The shrill trills of the whippoorwills seem obscene,
the gloss on their feathers shining proudly in the morning light,
flitting between the glossy green of the trees that
rustle now that their flowers have drifted off
      in a gentle confetti-storm.
The beauty that we wait for every year, cracked in the cold, is
wrong now.
Sure, it's on schedule,
but what is a schedule if every day is
the same ceiling at the same six a.m.
the same toast on the freezer-burned bread
the same mug clutched at the same kitchen table?
      Every night, when we draw the curtains closed
      I can't tell if it's yesterday
      or three months from now.
Shouldn't the sky replace the glitter of its sapphire
with the clouds of purple doom?
Shouldn't the cotton-candy sunsets
be aflame with smoke?
Where is the sickly green of nuclear waste and villainy
promised by all of the movies we used to watch?

As the World Burns

The creatures are singing lullabies while we scream into the
    void.
The freckles are popping out on my arms as a thousand ants
    on a restless log.
Somebody has mixed up the two themes of apocalypse and
    paradise,
which would be a fireable offense if anybody were still in the
    director's chair for this year of hindsight.

Lately
L. Stevens

So
lately
I have been
kicking dandelions
instead of blowing to
make a wish

Don't Spit On My Father
Candice Louisa Daquin

He's older now
And you, with your armor of youth see
A man without value, nobody, nothing, walking down the road
Not someone's father.
You don't know
What he has lived or who
Lives for him
And without cause or thought
Maybe out of some swimming, stifling anger
Something storing like poison in your gut
Masticating in your mouth you spit at him
In a time of Covid one and nine, it's a bit like
A bullet.
Maybe that's your power
In which case I pity you
But confess
If I had been walking alongside my father when you ran past
    and spat at him
I too wouldn't have been very thoughtful
I would have lunged at you and hit you, hard.
Probably the stupidest thing anyone can do
In a time of pandemics and loosened sanity.
It shows really ...
The sorrow of these times. The perversion of what is right
The permission for wrong
And words are lost, exchanged by quiet rage
You with your spit and run. Me with my fantasies of violent
    rebuke.
Maybe you feared too. Maybe you were simply a thoughtless

71

stranger.

I don't know the answer to that. I do know

It's not the first time I would defend my father and not the last

It feels like we are de-evolving. It seems as if we have turned into bare boned clans.

And strangers become murderers and fire keeping us safe at night.

I am a little woman, my father is tall. I make him laugh over the phone when he tells me about you

I describe flying through the sky with ninja moves. I even make the sound effects. WAAAA!!!

I love the sound of my dad's laughter. I have not seen him for two years. His laughter

Hides my tendency to want to cry with shame and regret

At the thought of a stranger spitting at my father

The proffer of small keen violence in the yawning, yellow teeth time of Covid one and nine.

Palm Sunday, 2020, New York
Rob Plath

as the daffodils
stand unbuckling
in the sun

as the dogs bark
at a couple
of strangers
stretching their
legs in the street

as owners graffiti
hopeful slogans
on plywood-covered
storefronts

as the museums
remain empty

as the morgues
overflow into
refrigerated
trucks

Plague

as cloistered
in rooms
we await
the terrible
apex
our hearts
die for
june

a monster under the bed
Erik Klingenberg (nightpoet)

how strange it feels these days to walk out
the door not knowing what danger lies on a
doorknob or a handrail, or a stranger's breath,
wondering if what you touch next might just
be a sentence of a slow and painful death,
it's almost like being in combat, waiting for
that one bullet with your name written on it
to strike home and blow your brains out,
or when you were a child and late at night
you quivered beneath the covers afraid to
move because you were so certain that
there was a monster under the bed. . .

my only visitor
Rob Plath

in the home
that holds
the old
& the sick
& the dying
staff closed
all the doors
on two floors
five times
this week
twenty times
this month
but many
of the old
& the sick
& the dying
are not fooled
know what's
going on
on the other
side of those
closed doors
as they lay
there waiting
wondering who
it is this time
while the only thing
only sure thing

As the World Burns

in their lives
is staff closing
all their doors
more & more
closed doors
as the only
visitor allowed
enters a room
another room
so many rooms

Walk on the Wild Side
Liz DeGregorio

We're walking in a field,
       wide-open spaces,
           bright blue above,
               birds chirping.

We're in a dream,
       no people around,
           no cars,
               no sirens.

We come to the top of a hill
       and cautiously remove our masks,
           feeling the sun warm our faces,
               upturned to the sky.

We hear voices approaching,
       then quickly don our masks,
           once again protected from the air,
               strangers, each other.

Disabled in The Plague
Sammie Payne

I sit secluded,
By fear and death,
Upon my neck I feel,
Mortality's breath.

I dare not venture,
Wander or roam,
Outside of this prison,
That I call a home.

On the rare occasion,
I pluck up the courage,
Harsh looks of judgment,
Do hurt and discourage.

They don't understand,
My war with my mask,
They assume I am selfish,
And refuse the task.

So back to my home,
I quickly retreat,
Hoping that soon,
Life won't be so bleak.

Quarantine, Night 14
Jamie L. Smith

Past midnight my whippoorwill-mind dips
dark wings into wonder— what if
I'm wrong and the birthmark

on my left thigh is a mole
morphing into Texas-shaped carcinoma?
Would my insurance cover that magic?

What if I really do
want children, some green-shuttered home
in gated community, complete

with a dented silver SUV? What if he's
re-elected? Maybe the phosphates
in my off-brand conditioner

really are doing damage to my scalp,
the earth, all of it. Dark feathered hair slips
down her back when she rises,

and is it wrong I replay
that spilling-down-moment when she lifts
from her wicker chair

when I can't sleep? She strides
to the bathroom where she lathers, repeats, leaves
my cheap shampoo uncapped.

As the World Burns

What if I said, You left it uncapped
again, didn't you? Maybe we
would snicker ourselves to sleep,

but I screw the top on the bottle,
the toothpaste, the lotion, wind up
my music-box-song of wrongs

'til dawn stills my whippoorwill.

To Run, No Chance to Dream
Irma Do

Sweat drips down
my brow,
my chin,
my arms,
my back
Onto the treadmill that has had better owners
it rumbles
it squeaks
it grinds
it whines
But it can't be heard up two flights of stairs at 3 AM
it won't disturb my quietly sleeping children
it won't disturb my quietly snoring spouse
it won't disturb the quiet illusion of life as it should be
Here in the basement cave with its napoleon ceiling
I do not want to sleep
I do not want to dream
I do not want to figure out how to stay safe from something that
can't be seen
I do not want to figure out a "new normal"
If I am moving, I am not dreaming
of things that I can't control
of things that I shouldn't hope for
of things that could be or should be
of things that start with "what if"
So I run but not away, just enough to sleep
without dreaming
without pretense

As the World Burns

without aspirations
without the energy for my brain to continue the run

It is now 5 AM.

Before Anxiety
Jennifer Carr

I would say I am sorry
I can't come into work today
but the truth is…
I'm not really sorry
because I grew tired of the hospital job
the long 12-hour shifts
the overnight shifts
stress of the emergency room
the possibility of contracting COVID-19
how my mind is controlled
by a new stressor
latched onto a new challenge
of returning to journalism
a reporter as I once was
20 years ago
but now reporting on the current events
the latest COVID-19 updates
drama of local city council
corrupt city council members
every once in a while
lucky enough to find a light-hearted feature story
I'm able to breathe for a moment
and I remember what life was like before anxiety

The Mask
L. Stevens

Call me what you will
Never forget you made me
to protect you from what kills
Call me what you will
a shield, a shroud, still
no guarantee
Call me what you will
Never forget. You made me

Park Panic Attack

Liz DeGregorio

Last night, I climbed
fifteen sets of stairs in the park.

It wasn't the deep humidity
        or the actual exercise
that made me sit down at the top
        and panic quietly—

Or quietly enough
that the only other person around,
        a man singing off-key to himself,
failed to notice my gasps for clean air.

I pulled down my mask,
        the thick air filling my lungs
        and giving me surprising relief.
I smelled the grass, the trees, my own skin.

Tears ran down my face,
mixing with a sheen of sweat,
        and stinging my eyes.
I looked into the trees,
        and my heart was momentarily full.

It Has Come to This
Rachael Z. Ikins

Final Breaths
Devika Mathur

There is a strange occurrence of days now
with seeds of pain swinging under my thin curtains.
Strange voices deplete my limbs,
a flower trying to bloom.
I see, a star trying to seduce
old afternoons sit and watch me struggling,
trying to put up my screams for humans,
my screams so orange for the climate.
There is an absolute sick horror now,
gazing upon my empty mind.
The rooms are not as pure as before,
a scream of a woman prevails,
a scream about equality exists.
Amidst the pandemic,
I see my home burning,
my people uttering words about prayers,
prayers, that suffice the shadow of humanity
prayers, that entwine the slick game of Gods.
I fidget watching my place burns,
I evaporate into tiny droplets of sky
only to become a soft breeze on the wounded hearts.

unusually calm in a crisis
Melita White

I am
unusually calm
in a crisis
A crisis is normal
to me—
danger my oxygen
detachment my friend
we hold hands
and freeze at the centre
blank, numb
and hopefully not too stupid

This day
like every other
is just another to survive
and I have weathered worse

I am an expert
in crisis
I know what I need to do
I've lived my life
being one step ahead
outrunning death
while she slashes at my heels
inflicting wounds
but never taking me

Plague

My life is at risk
and this is just normal
A crisis is normal
to me—
I know it will pass
as it always has
as it always does
for me

Benign

Nadia Garofalo

My skin is too thin to stomach it
you know, anything

Wind, rain, snow
hands, mouths, blows

Tears
micro and macro
superficial
deep

Never terminal
not yet anyway

Small Comforts
Destiny Killian

When society overwhelms
and anxiety hammers against my ribcage
I escape
tap, tap, tap, tap
My fingers drum against the keyboard
electronic entrance to a world
made of sensations
My mind its sole inhabitant
instead of homes or
looming landscapes
small comforts paint a paradise
of quiet ideals
Laptop humming in tune
with the cat warming my side
I inhale
the smell of paper & ink pen
of leather worn and true
books bringing with them the presence
of familiar friends
sharp and ever-efficient Times New Roman
cuts through to all that matters
While whipped cream and chocolate drizzle
floating atop a monochrome mug
warms my black coffee heart

Fragments of a Perfect Whole
Merril D. Smith

"It seems impossible that their calm should ever return or that
we should ever compose from their fragments a perfect whole
or read in the littered pieces the clear words of truth."
–Virginia Woolf, *To the Lighthouse*

The world seems broken—
fragments scatter on howling winds
I stand in the eye of the storm, calm—

here, each day lasts a week
each week lasts a year,
then it's over in a blink

like the world existing in a puddle,
where the sun illuminates the rippling trees
but only at the right angle, then disappears

as clouds drift together and apart
and trees reach up to touch them,
I stand and watch

as they float by
in a corona sky,
and I'm waiting

for the storm to pass—
for the scent of bright green grass
carried on a soft spring breeze

Plague

with robin trill
and mockingbird's song—
a chorus,

fragments of a perfect whole—
notes in nature's symphony, where birth's piccolo is followed by
death's snare drum, a coda that repeats,

and life continues, perhaps not a song, but a puzzle
with random pieces missing,
knocked from the table by a cosmic cat's paw

to be found in another time, another path, the road
not taken. Truth--the design mostly complete; beauty still
recognizable—
perhaps that's enough.

That Buoyant World
Candice Louisa Daquin

You are afraid to shut the front door
it is an unblinking eye to the living
you are attached to a virus, like a fly
stuck firm in ointment, will
be claimed slow and sure
by its urge to escape, it shall
sink deeper and knowing this, you
refuse to close away the day, but
by standing against urging cold air
feeling labored breath of all those
who maintain and climb their days into years
by the touch of their effort, and the rise and fall
of that buoyant world
you shall rejoin the wheel as it arcs and spins
counting down our mortal pieces
such as we are, labored by knowing
how fragile the shimmer of life
yet, not yet, yet
we are still
afloat

Quarantine

Andrew McDowell

All activity halted
Stuck at home
If outside
Wear a mask
Stand six feet apart
Else in danger
For others
For yourself
Nowhere to go
Nothing to do
Can we reflect?
Can we ponder?
Can we turn inward?
Maybe
Maybe not
In the instant
People want
Spoiled
Impatient
Think again
What matters most
Never
Never
Take for granted
Again

Nevertheless
Jessica Jacobs

This time is sacred for the good or bad
it could become but isn't yet. For the 4 a.m. phone
that doesn't ring but might.

Ma nishtana ha'laila ha'zeh mi-kol ha'leilot?
Why is this night different than all other nights?

It's not. It's only the cusp each night is, the anteroom
for all that follows—illness, one step
off the wrong curb, one moment when the heart forgets
to keep time.
                    But such questions are essential,
inviting the story that takes us from slavery to freedom.

Even when celebrating Passover alone, we are commanded
to ask, to become both the teller and the other
to whom the story is told:

And the night of the final plague,
mark your doorposts with blood
so the Angel of Death might pass over.

Then we eat bitter herbs to taste the pain of those not
passed by.

And there was a loud cry in the land, for there was
no house where there was not
someone to mourn.

Plague

In hope some trace remains,
I run my hands along every doorway
we enter, wondering,
    Why others and not us?
I know nothing that makes us worthy
of such consideration.

                    And dread, sometimes, is a darkness
so thick it has me groping at noon. And questions,
sometimes, are all we have left: Like even with all
that could, that *will* occur, what else is there
                    except to move forward?

So I Speak with Ancestors
Sean Heather McGraw

So I speak with Ancestors.
I feel *hoh-mód*, anxiety, as anxious as a tree before an axe.
Being a historian, it's hard not to see the parallels
between the plague now and the plagues that have already
    been.
There are so many new words now—
COVID-19, zoom, face covering, social distancing.

It's all so isolating—but isolation is where we want to be.
I'm already an introvert, so some of this is familiar,
A life of rarely talking to people, staying home, reading ancient
    texts
In Old English, Old Norse, Old Irish, Latin, Greek, German.

Hoh-mód, anxiety that the pandemic will never cease
And that I may never see my family again who live on the other
Side of the continent.
Anxiety that I will get this voracious beast
Especially since soon I will have to go back to teach.

This virus is like a ravening monster, it is *giefer* - gluttonous -
Like the Big Bad Wolf and of course, since childhood,
I've always been Little Red Riding Hood
(my mother sent me my little red cape which I wore constantly)

And we have been so *latian*—so slow, so late,
In defending ourselves from this new Grendel, the great
    monster
In the ancient poem Beowulf, the one who devoured warriors

Plague

every night.
Where is a new Beowulf? This tiny monster can barely be
   seen.
It's almost invisible and yet so strong. He fought the monster,
   his mother and a dragon.
He kept his people safe from the terrors of war, greed, gluttony.

I have now gone three times to that strange land where
There is a *prass* - a parade - of nurses, lined up with cotton-
   swabs,
Ready to stick into one nostril and then the other,
My eyes well up in tears and my nose wants to sneeze.
But I'd rather that then get this dreadly disease.

On heofenum - in the heavens - where is the God that
   promised deliverance
To the ancient Israelites from their disease if they but looked up
   to the
Brass Serpent—they would be healed.
Our doctors and nurses wear such brass serpents on their
   clothes,
They now are those sent to heal and yet the monster yields up
   its secret belly slow
It doesn't want, like the dragon, to be slain in the underbelly, as
   Beowulf slew him.

This virus is like a *hondwyrm* - hand worm - reptile or insect—
As it creeps fast through peoples, tribes, kin, clans, nations,
   kingdoms.
The world is a scary place to be, so maybe it's good I'm
   already an introvert
Reading my ancient texts, preparing my lectures.
Yet, still they seem to know already what I am going through,

As the World Burns

I cannot avoid the fate of the world—fear, hopelessness, anger,
    anxiety.

As I live in *middangeard* - middle earth - where are the
    sorcerers and elves
To help us fight this ancient and tiny beast?
Scientists and doctors are the new sorcerers and elves.
So in my *nosu* – nose – the swabs go.
You see - students - how already you speak Old English,
The language of the ancestors.

As a historian, I sit with the dead ancestors all the day and
    night.
My ancestors in the British Isles and Scandinavia,
your ancestors, in Africa, Asia, Europe, the Americas,
the ancestors of those who live on the other side of the world
all ancestors are equally alive to me.

And all ancestors seem to chant, it matters not how, nor when,
But you will all be next to us someday and then you'll see
How we are all alike, but you—"*God sceal wið yfele*" –
Good must fight with evil, God must fight with evil.

I ask my *bodig* every day - how does my body feel?
Any symptoms? I already have health issues.
Eagan, muð, earan, hnecca, hrycg, eaxl, earm, hand, finger,
    scanca, fet.
Eyes, mouth, ears, neck, back, shoulder, arm, hand, finger, leg,
    feet.
Every nurse asks when I go to an appointment.

Plague

When I was young, I was idealistic and hoped I could change
    the world.
Do students listen? Does anyone listen now?
I still speak with the ancestors and apologize for my
    generation,
Our *hatian* - hate- our violence, our unkindness, our
    quickness to judge,
our willingness to take no thought for others,
our selfish demands that harm another.

Once I had a student call me up years after, to ask for help in a
    serious matter
I was amazed he thought of me, history it seems is almost no
    one's favorite subject
So hard to understand, dates and names and events, reasons
    why.
But good must fight with evil, I still teach through those dates
    and names and events.

I read my grandfather's story yesterday, him talking about his
    father, his grandfather.
The small acts that become great things, Elijah Paul, a
    southern Baptist preacher and farmer
In a town where every white man was a member of the Ku Klux
    Klan,
They did not ask him to join. He built a school for the black
    children,
And helped their parents have good houses on his land.

He never knew his father, who left to fight in the Civil War, and
    died when he was a baby.
He *lufode* – loved – his wife and child, yet felt he had to fight
    against those he thought

As the World Burns

Might take his land from him. What Paul thought of slavery, we
   do not know, it is not recorded.
I imagine the advice he might have given his son from the
   grave.

Like Beowulf, he fought what he thought was a monster to save
   his people.
Go, son, and do likewise, whatever monsters you feel are there
   beside you.
Elijah Paul fought, in his way, the monsters that he saw beside
   him.

My grandfather, who served in the Army from 1936 to 1963,
   and even overseas.
Fought too, against the monsters of his time, and never
   wavered.
In my time there are so many monsters, perhaps that is true of
   all times.
Even in this social distancing isolation I have a chance to fight
   a monster.

Metamorphosis
Cynthia L. Bryant

A sadness has fallen
Like an escalator ride
Into madness

Cheap cotton masks
Disposal latex gloves
Worn with sweats

A seed has been
planted and another
And another

Day in   Day in
Life resides deep
Inside, incubation

Earth Mother
cleansed, refreshed
In people-less spring

Thousands of dead
will be grieved, buried
in parks temporarily

Millions hang in
restless chrysalis of
their design, making

Will tomorrow
Find us broken spirits
Or reborn butterflies

What I Discovered in the Pandemic
Kim Harvey

"Thirsty people will find shiny things beautiful,"
　　Something Jane Hirshfield said on *Science Friday.* Poets
are magpies collecting images, scraps of words, a turn

of phrase overheard then tucked away for future use.
　　Random facts, like the first woman to cycle around the world
learned to ride a bike just hours before she set off.

Vervet monkeys make different sounds to warn of leopards,
　　eagles & snakes. One shriek sends the other monkeys
　　　scurrying,
another has them gazing skyward or down at their feet.

A title I keep in my back pocket: *Now a Low-Grade Fever.*
　　Something Heather said in Napa when we were delirious
from so little sleep, so much poetry & wine. "You are the
　　power."

Another line that hasn't found its time. What I've seen
　　on my way to work: pink poster about a lost puppy,
text alert—missing senior, someone's sofa on the curb.

I once had a sofa like that, the first one I bought as an adult.
　　Trump Sucks, carved into the sidewalk. Did you know
a jellyfish has no brain & a cuttlefish has three hearts?

Plague

I learned that while riding BART, something I never thought I'd
    miss.
   Bowie said artists were the original false gods. Remember
this: dogs need amino acids like taurine, cysteine &
    methionine.

You never know when you'll want to use that in a line.
   The things I carried through the pandemic.
Or the things that carried me. Maybe all poems are questions.

Previously published by The Shore

Famine

In the First Week of a New Decade, Humanity Stands Singed

After the political tension between Iran and the United States in the first week of 2020
Megha Sood

Not a week has gone by and I smell the blistering taste
of my dreams, my desires,
my mornings,
my hopes,
as an aftertaste
the unending hunger of humankind
at the back of my throat

this revenge of monstrous proportions
this boisterous rage,
this chest-thumping attitude
has been a curse
if only God could tell,
break his silence for once
for the benefit of mankind

On the verge to obliterate
each and every small hope
desires and wishes birthing in the palm of a child
hope resting carelessly
on the end of a curved smile
waiting on the fallen eyelashes
ready to make a wish sublime

Famine

This inveterate hunger can't be doused
by a territorial declaration
where boundaries are nothing
but a limitation of mankind
to share anything which is
pure and true

Like Nature
Like monsoon dance of the peacocks,
Like the wings of a monarch,
Like a symphony,
Like a serenade,
Like all good things lost and forgotten

These lines reek of blood,
war, death, starvation, and loneliness
these lines are not marking our possessions
these likes are
Cutting,
slashing,
slicing our dreams in halves
bleeding on both ends unbidden

Here at the start of the decade,
humanity stands parched
humanity stands singed.

Last to Know
Nayana Nair

I regret to tell you this
that the blue sky that you died for
is no longer blue.
It is painting its face with remains
of our greed, with the colors of our wars.
But it is still sort of fair.
It is trying hard not to choose sides,
not to become the flags that unite
only those whose favorite words are
'future', 'safety', 'money', 'greatness',
while they clutch in their hands the fate of people
they don't identify with-
'burden' they call them.
They are the new gods
that we are no longer allowed to call out or even mock.
I have lost every bit of my passive aggressiveness.
Life has become more bearable
now that my skin is not broken for making too much noise,
now that we have learnt to hold each other's tongue
so that we may not lose more friends than we already have.
I regret to tell you
that your dreams will remains dreams
and you might be one of the last to know
how dreams felt in your eyes,
how tomorrows used to change by effort.

Redbird
Allie Nelson

And the seasons turn, cherries to tomatoes to pumpkin orange.

There is not much constant in nature but effervescent change,
like how lemons taste on the tongue, or the path of hurricanes.

Even the laws of gravity get suspended sometimes, and love
is an old book in a New England parish that has seen better
days, all antiquated rust on the locket inside it of your great
aunt, farms to marrow of skyscrapers, tradition to upstarts to
a lack of faith the youth seem so content with.

But I fear God,
and I am the bones of winter, and it is only in planting beauty
that we can hope to reap the corn and sow spring, what regret
these ghost towns have in the Appalachians,

the run of the meat
is hickory, best smoke it long and get washed out to sea, paint
    the
fence white, and build your dwelling on the village green so you
are the center of attention,

twist and turn at a soc hop like it's your
grandparent's malt shop dream, sweet teeth, in me are leaves
    of
hauntings, and to fall from a sycamore and swing from an oak
is but the path of angels lit on fire with the coming
    Thanksgiving,

As the World Burns

my cup runneth over, it never satisfies me, as four and twenty
blackbirds fly and the scarecrow rots. But that is just a rumor,
and the truth of me is dusty lace and spiced cider, let's die
   together
then burst green in May, immortality, transformation, harrows.

In the county church, there is an old grandmother bowed over.

Were that I had her constance.

It is enough
Petru J Viljoen

It's South Africa. It's winter, a particularly cold one (for South Africa). It's a very small town, ravaged by Covid-19. Hunger prevails. A thousand had to be fed by less than a handful. The chat group was ablaze last night. Where are the food parcels? Tempers soared … and soured. A leader, in charge, peeved. Believe it!

Yes but, and then that, but you … but where did the food parcels go then? The rich and well off sit and sip illicit liquor in the sun, arranging themselves for after (Covid). They gathered in God's name. So where are the food parcels!

But if you did and if they didn't … and then they put up the electricity charges. And still no-one says about the missing food parcels. Those who still could now can't cook any longer unless they make a fire in the yard. A household of ten to eat from one granny's social grant. One fire, one teacup worth of food, once a day. A small child has been crying non-stop for two days. It's God's Will. No food parcels. Be patient 'they' say.

Calling out, just, just short of being called names (on the chat group). Fingers pointing, pointed back, yes but you … whatever … where are the goddamn food parcels!!

the heat of the moment

passed—I draw the blankets

up to my chin

No More Kissing in Paris
Maria Gray

The Louvre is closed. No more kissing in Paris.
New York City's uninsured are interred on Hart Island, and

in Iran, the burial pits are visible from space. My brain sinks
into its stem, a sunflower unwilling to bear the weight

of her own blossom. Corona is Latin for crown. I keep revisiting
Coho's rendition of the seven-year fire: the way apples baked

on trees; how animals were incinerated on the spot, streams
boiled; how the northwest rose like a rabid phoenix from its
funeral, how

yellow buses of schoolchildren took field trips to replant
the forests, how government officials dropped seeds from
helicopters,

something they'd never tried before. Crown fire like a squirrel
bounding from treetop to treetop. Someone I love will die,

probably. Someone who dies will have loved me,
or would have. I am stuck inside this house

forever, in labor with the world I carry
like a child, like a tumor. I drove and then I stopped.

I listened, then I left. The day is still bright, and
we are so young. We have our whole lives

ahead of us.

A Year Turned Inside Out
Cynthia L. Bryant

So many years
spent in the waiting room
Before now

Practicing
The art of holding
My breath

So quiet
That I dared not be heard
Or seen

Coming out on occasion
To practice identity of
Whom I heard I was

All of this comes
Back to me in black and white
In times of tribulation despair

The isolation of COVID-19
Is where I live
Have always lived

The years of ripping off skin
Layer by layer to find me
Who I might be

A clear reflection today
Once lost in pus and puke
I see it all

As the World Burns

Surrounded in fat like a shield
The fear has risen
Hangs in the air a frozen scream

The return of daily chaos
An unknown enemy
Ready to wrestle me down

Is this what happens
Before death descends
Inventory of life never lived

Just under the surface

Velma Hamilton

Just under the surface
No one can see
The eruption of darkness
No one can see
Me trying to breathe
Trying to claw my way out

Just under the surface
There are things I cannot describe
The things that haunt my mind
Things I can no longer bear

Just under the surface
I weep for that which I long for, that which I had but for only a
    moment
A weeping I cannot control
A fight I cannot win
A fight I do not wish to fight any longer

Just under the surface
There is no peace
There is no joy
You don't know me
You can't imagine my despair

On the surface
I am strong
Self-assured
I'm happy

As the World Burns

On the surface
You will never believe
You will shake your self-righteous judgmental heads in disbelief
You will call me names such as coward and crazy and other
    things,

But,

Just under the surface
I died a long time ago
So long ago I can't remember
My body just needed to catch up to my soul.
At last it has

What rips us apart, lies…
Just under the surface

Identity
Katherine DeGilio

This is me. It's who I am—but it's not *me*.
Do you understand?

Where battles fall and I pick up the rubble to make pet rocks,
I am doing my best to make a home between the cracks in the
    glass,
but I am not where the light shifts in, I am a part of the
    building—and yet I am not.

You walk through it, and take yourself down elevators of
    identity
and you know you belong there.
I am riding the wave expecting it to jolt.

Will I be thrown down at any possible moment?

So, instead of taking refuge where I am not certain,
I place pride in the withering leaves, because they are mine.
But that doesn't mean I don't want to be you.

Why can't I be both? Me and *me*—you, me, you? Is that not
    true?

Right now, I am assuming my label, to allow myself the dietary
    restriction.
But one day, I would love to just to go to the party,
enjoy the salvaged conversations beside condiments we can
    all enjoy.
Can I not eat at the table and choose my own portion?
Or must we all partake in the same to be invited?

She will not let me go
Kristiana Reed

The wind calls me its friend and I believe it.
The trees look at me with their knotted eyes
and I nod beneath their grand omniscience.
I realise I cannot vanish.
Gaia's grip is nondescript, effervescent and
ever-present. She will not let me go.
She will not allow me to descend into titanic depths
and consort with Kronos and the like.
She kisses my temples and tells me life on Earth
is feet grounded upon the earth not beneath it.
I realise being buried alive is not a blessing.
I realise I will leave marks wherever I go:
footprints, oily fingerprints, long auburn hair
strewn like war-time debris, the sound of my voice—
quiet and loud—, whispered breaths.
I realise Gaia has built me a home in which
I must build my own. My body is a home.
Not a temple. Not a train-wreck.
Not an answer to all of your prayers.
But a small home with cobwebs and lintels
in need of dusting, with sloping floors
and single-glazed windows, with a fire
burning and a draught beneath the doors.
I realise happiness is woven through with sadness,
and regret only means something if you frame it,
keep it above your mantelpiece and admire it
as if it were a Monet or a Constable.
I realise my too many possessions have shaped me;

Famine

whittled me like wood into a woman
who wishes to vanish, but never should.
I realise love is an interminable ache.

The trees watch me with knotted eyes
and I close mine, to sleep.

Upon Waking in a Pandemic
Christine E. Ray

if this be
the end of days
it is not just the world
that has become
unrecognizable
it is me I find
most changed
I thought
I knew myself
oil burning furiously
upon the water
fist raised in defiance
challenging the
heartless gods
only to find myself
instead
drifting rootless
unmoored
in this dark sea
time
barely able to muster
the drive
energy
to stand on raised toes
face tilted toward
the sun
inhale deeply
breathe

Dead Wrong / you will say I thought she was fine
Velma Hamilton

You will say I thought she was fine...

I feel it inside with such intensity
It's as if I'm on a runaway train but powerless to jump off

It calls to me with an internal voice so strong, whispering do it!
    Just do it and be free.
It's all I want and all I think about.

You will say I thought she was fine...

I think about it with every free thought
Planning the ways
How can it look like an accident
Does it really matter
I've done my homework
I've thought of every detail

You'll say I thought she was fine...

I lie now to everyone around me
I smile bigger
I laugh harder
I say I'm great even before you ask just so it seems more
    Convincing
No detail will be overlooked

As the World Burns

You'll say I thought she was fine...

The time is drawing near
The whispers are now screams
I want it so bad
You couldn't begin to imagine
I wouldn't want you to

You'll say I thought she was fine...

This is not your cross to bear
This is not your concern
It is my peace I seek
It is my salvation to find
My love was strong
My will was not

Yes, you were wrong
dead wrong
I was not fine

Choice Perhaps
Jane Dougherty

Is this the way to better days,
the isolation of meadow grass
and the slipping into bird silence,
the watching and listening,
the not owning,

venturing into town like the foxes and pigeons,
warily, darting for what we need and retreating,
tending trees and the tender lives of fragile flowers,
stepping aside when the deer pass
and the badger blunders?

Is this more admirable than doing the shops
and sipping coffee on a café terrace,
wandering bright streets early morning
when the stars are blinded by the light,
or is it a fiction,

there can be no going back,
jet trails are the new blue,
and the wanting novelty,
ever-changing, like the commercial light play on the tower
is for ever and ever amen?

I have no answer, only for me,
but the tears for what is dying
are lit by the steady stream of car headlamps,
blurring the bloodied fur,
lying far from home on the hard shoulder.

Skipping The Seasons
S.A. Quinox

I see them. The faces of those who have
already come to pass. Mourning shadows,
walking sore inside weary clothes.
Afraid to breathe as the air has grown
to be as toxic as the hearts peeling from
the circles sleeping sound beneath their eyes.
Touch has grown to be a thing from the past now.
The gentle yearning they once felt for
their own kind has come to grow toxic with it.
Like leaves plucked from the trees during
a mid-summer week that has suddenly
transitioned into an aching winter,
skipping the gentle touch of autumn,
and never facing the glory of spring.

After the Election
November 9, 2016
Jessica Jacobs

This summer, for the first time in eighty years,
June's full moon—that strawberry, honey,

planting moon—rose to meet
the summer solstice: the day of greatest light

bound to the night of greatest light
for the only time

in our lifetime. So after dinner and dancing,
we stepped naked into the sea

where the only warmth was my wife's body
against mine, making a shivering perch of my thighs.

Whatever lurked those waters, we turned
toward the sky, toward the light's

soft falling on the waves, and away
from the death of that long summer:

black man after black man after black man
murdered, bombs in airports, the forty-nine

in my hometown of Orlando who'd never again
catch their own eyes

As the World Burns

in a dance club mirror and wonder
what the night ahead
might bring, even that TV madman grabbing
for power we couldn't imagine

he'd win, all of it
gave way to the moon

on the wind-threshed water—the light shattered
and therefore multiplied.
Now, looking back

from this aftermath, what does it mean
to know such a moment

is over, to try and accept it will not return?
That night, we surrendered

to radiance, drank in as much good light
as we could. Can any of that flickering still live

inside us? And if it does, how must we break
open to let it shine again?
Now, when

that day, remembered, is a mausoleum
with all the lights left on,

will every day of every year
that follows hold a little less

Famine

brightness, darkness steadily reclaiming
ground? Can we ever again avert our eyes,

for even an instant, from history
to give ourselves to beauty?
Perhaps we shouldn't; but I want to.

Thirteen Ways of Looking at Life Before the Virus
Lesléa Newman

I.
I remember shaking hands:
damp sweaty hands and dry scratchy hands,
bone-crushing handshakes and dead-fish handshakes,
two-handed handshakes, my hand sandwiched
between a pair of big beefy palms.
I remember hairy hands and freckled hands,
young smooth hands and old wrinkled hands,
red-polished fingernails and bitten-jagged fingernails,
stained hands of hairdressers who had spent all day dyeing,
dirty hands of gardeners who dug down deep into the good
earth.

II.
Thousands of years ago, a man stuck out his right hand
to show a stranger he had no weapon.
The stranger took his hand and shook it
to make sure he had nothing up his sleeve.
And that is how it began.

III.
I remember sharing a bucket
of greasy popcorn with a boy
at the movies
(though I no longer remember
the boy or the movie)
the thrill of our hands
accidentally on purpose
brushing each other in the dark.

133

Famine

IV.
I remember my best girlfriend
and I facing each other to play
a hand-clapping game, shrieking
"Miss Mary...Mack! Mack! Mack!"
and the loud satisfying *smack!*
as our four palms slapped.

V.
I remember high fives
and how we'd laugh when we missed
and then do a do-over.

VI.
I remember the elegant turn
of shiny brass doorknobs
cool to the touch.

VII.
I remember my mother's hands
tied to the railings of her hospital bed
and how I untied them
when the nurse wasn't looking
and held them in my lap.

VIII.
I remember holding my father's hand
how the big college ring he wore
rubbed against my birthstone ring
and irritated my pinky
but I never pulled away.

As the World Burns

IX.
I remember the joy of offering
my index finger to a new baby
who wrapped it in her fist
as we gazed at each other in wonder.

X.
I remember tapping a stranger
on the shoulder and saying,
"Your tag is showing.
Do you mind if I tuck it in?"
She didn't mind. I tucked it in.

XI.
I remember salad bars and hot bars.
I remember saying, "Want a bite?"
and offering a forkful
of food from my plate.
I remember asking ,"Can I have a sip?"
and placing my lips
on the edge of your cold frosty glass.

XII.
I remember passing around the Kiddush cup,
each of us taking a small sip of wine.
I remember passing around the challah,
each of us ripping off a big yeasty hunk.
I remember picking up a serving spoon
someone had just put down
without giving it a second thought.

Famine

XIII.
I remember sitting with a mourner
at a funeral, not saying a word,
simply taking her hand.

"Thirteen Ways of Looking at Life Before the Virus" first appeared in
New Verse News, March 31, 2020.

When I walk out of this glass door called Covid...
Dr. Sneha Rooh

When I walk out of this glass door, the glass door, the glass door, the glass door, I'd reach you instantly I know. Like in thought, because I've been thinking of you a lot. I would reach outside your home where there are two chairs to sit and where we watched the street. Did you know that we wouldn't be able to share the same room for months when you said you didn't have the time to meet me last Sunday? Anyway, I would give you a hug and rest my cheek on your neck and let it grow warm. I would take time to look at you when I looked into your eyes. I would hold your hand and smile, because it would be the first time we are holding hands. You wouldn't be scared to infect your mother after meeting me. I wouldn't fear taking any infection to the immune-compromised patients in the ward. We would talk about the last time we didn't touch and how long ago the last time was.

When I walk through this glass door called Covid.

To the Huggers
Amie Campbell

To my friend who hugs too hard, too long-

I am sorry for every time I wiggled out of a hug before you were done.

I apologize for every "too tight" I squeaked out.

You've respected my space and acknowledged that I am less a hugger than you, and
while I appreciated that in the moment,

I now regret every hug I ever missed out on.

I lament not joining you went you went in for that fourth hug the last time we said good-
bye.

I did not know it would be so long until we could embrace again.

I mourn all these hug-less months without you.

For now, we must stay apart,

But I promise I will have the biggest, tightest hug waiting for you when we meet again.

Skin Hunger
Philip A. Wardlow

If you had told me I would have
yearned for a simple handshake,
months from now,
I would have scoffed at such a silly notion.

If you would have said a hug from
a loved one was a distant memory
and that only through dreaming in bed
at night could such an implausible embrace happen,
I would have laughed in your face.

No light touches, no manly shoulder to shoulder hugs,
no holding hands, no fist bumps,
no incidental brushing of skin against
skin in the everyday going on
of life.
None of that.

I am bereft and unaware of the warmth
or coldness of a cheek or simple palms of another,
stolen is the smile behind
a mask that might have touched my soul
as they looked my way in the incidental
happenings of a mere
day.

Famine

There is a gnawing
Deep
A pang
Inside
Screaming
A hunger threatening to consume
To feel
To know
the innocent intimate touch
in all the little ways lives seek to connect.

As the World Burns

We cried a long time ago. We don't cry anymore.
Candice Louisa Daquin

A warbling, holding, green glass pain
like joined hands make paper cut
invisible like girl in crowd, falls
deep as ink without light
stinging with clamoring cymbal
tears almost bare themselves as first night lovers, tremorous
retreat beyond the naked streets
it is not brutal gnashing strength
but soft lipped resignation
a little eclipsing hope
for bare faced easement
lain like prayers and rushes and thrown flowers wetting paving
    stones
no ceremony. Only, black cars devoid of dust
a trail without salt. They bent lower to seek. Not yet.
it's hard to say it. The wind chokes words. Before.
We walk on. Omphalos in fatigued lament
toward reprieve, illuminate in muted tempest.

Famine

When I am, play me recordings of those I loved, while I'm
Deirdre Fagan

I made bread for you as we baked.
Dinners were divine.

We checked our numbers, our temps,
Our coughs as we popped allergy meds.

At night we watched movies when we were spent.
Read when we were in need of escape.

And we considered our odds,
Like bettors at a blackjack table in Vegas.

While we played poker with the children,
Each upping our ante, trying to guess at our hands.

If I make it and you don't, "Call an auctioneer."
If you make it and I don't, "Keep the books and paintings."

The eldest, just shy of 18, we all decided,
Could raise his sister.

The two banter about who gets the "master suite,"
Allowing the reason to recede.

At night we drink love. We don't pray because
We don't pray.

As the World Burns

We peer into the abyss of each other's eyes, and know
Everything is fleeting.

Even this, and we embrace again.
Again, we embrace.

The lights go out when that's all we can take.
When we are done.

Just before giving into sleep, I ask you to play
The recordings of those I loved, while I'm.

Tomorrow Behind Closed Eyes
Karissa Whitson

We wake the same
In beds made with sweaty sheets
As the animals cry through the night
We wake the same
The ground around us sinking as it always has, but more
Never felt under the weight it is today
We wake the same
No longer to leave the door open to let in morning air
No longer to go out to see the ones we love most
We wake the same
With dancing images of idealist worlds floating through our
    heads
As the world around us closes itself around us
We wake the same
Suffocating under the pressure of the world
Not making pearls but instead crushing people
We wake the same
In terror, as we never knew to exist in such a world that
    promises us the best
As it is now it will remain
We wake the same
And at the same time
We will never be the same again

Shelter In Place
Jamie L. Smith

Hands plunged in frothy hot dishwater
I successfully snap

another chip-resistant coffee cup
—*fantastic*—handle

split on the drain lip.
Saucer-eyed, my cat gives me

that look.
My red-wine-spill of expletives

cascades across the white-tiled counter
but I can't hear myself

over the electric sear and swell
mounting in my ears—*cicadas*.

Why today?
Emerald hail shot up from hell

so many summers late
those green-shelled screams resurface

rise and knock
their stiff little bodies hurled

Famine

against this house. The world's great cruelty—
it's clockwise.

Griefs silent
years beneath feet

unearth themselves and hum.

Cinders

Lindz McLeod

We have become islands;
limpets cabled together like
beaded, distant swords,
stabbing the length of a moment.
Preserve yourself, but don't pickle
in the loneliness of a
still-sunny afternoon.
Spend time with your beloved,
rejoin the world at your own pace.

Pour a cup out for the ones
you miss, I miss—how I miss you, boy,
asleep on my palm, with
soft paws curled in Gangnam style.
I lie still to conjure fur against skin;
I prolong the opening of
a door, to falsify belief that I might
find him sprawled on the floor,
innocent of the outer world
but delighted that his best friend is
home again. While bubbled breath
swells like uncooked batter,
and lighted cherries
stub out too soon
across the map. More than one
from my own contacts list.
And this rounded shape at
the foot of my bed, a grief-spark
that will never stop burning.

Eden
Rachel Finch

They haven't told me that's why my baby died.
I will not ask.

I was fourteen weeks when my body started slowing down,
when my chest tightened and I shivered and sweated and
    ached.

This was back when 'it's just a virus'
didn't carry the same weight,
heavy on our brains
and hearts.

I was fifteen weeks when I could sleep through the night
without catching my breath.
When the dog stopped resting his head on my belly.

I talked to the sky.
I talked to my body.
I talked to my womb.
And I knew.

I was seventeen weeks when they told me my son was dying.
I birthed him as he slept and left chunks of my
heart
in the hospital so he'd
never forget me.

I would have been 20 weeks when my chest closed over again.
My children dropped like flies around me
before 24 hours had passed, one
and then another one and
then another one and
another and we lay for six days, a silent room of fallen birds.

As the World Burns

This was back when 'it's just a virus' didn't carry the same
     weight,
heavy on our brains
and hearts.

I would have been 25 weeks when we first heard.
And I knew.

Soak
Nadia Garofalo

Press my fingers along the water
to feel the breaking of its skin
wherein and land meets

It's hard to mourn
the living
harder to hold
the dead

Over and over
pulling
over and over

There is no clear answer
no great lesson
beyond the ripples
we send
by our own hands

Eventually the ties break
the sound echoes
and little we can do
once the water turns tepid

april
dani bowes

i do not have a dry cough, but i am hacking
up sweet peas—april's flower. the vines
wrap around the pink of my throat
forcing me to gasp
for what? a birthday that does not
appear like a ghost sitting
six feet apart from siblings
in the backyard, candles blown out
by the wind—or an invisible death
i have not been infected yet
but the space between my sister's arms
and my partner's saltwater pine cologne
my pop pop's favorite sweater
is a slow execution.

A Condolence Call
Megha Sood

Grief sits like a day old soup in my kitchen unless the anger
   stirs it
rattles and boils it. Grief rises to the surface and chokes me

I hear the loss of a mother. My friend's mother, over the phone.
It's a condolence call yet I can't seem to join in his grief

Sudden loss disjoints your body, the pieces don't seem to fit
   anymore
Body and language are extricable. Our tongue moves in the
   way

our body can't decipher in grief. I can't seem to form a legible
   sentence
our conversation keeps coming back to the grocery, the
   loneliness of

being stuck in a condo looking over the lush green deserted
   parks.
I don't want to bring back the conversation of the dead and
   dying.

The whole thread of conversation is about feeding the ones we
   love.
Loss is pouring through the thin sluices of this city. Every damn
   day.

Which starts again the same way it ended yesterday. Or was it
   tomorrow?
With sidewalks pitted with the bones of the dead.

As the World Burns

I can't seem to fathom the desperation and anger in his voice
    of not being
able to visit her mother during her last times, the pain and the
    grief carry over

like a failing enjambment from one meaningless conversation
to another till we ran out of the small talk. The silences
    between

the pauses take the shape of the unsaid condolence, as I
    slowly hang up the phone.
There is no defined language for grief. Lesson learned.

Famine

213,928
COVID-19 deaths in the United States as of 10/9/2020
Christine E. Ray

knife clenched
in numb fingers
I carve vertical lines
into white plaster
that crumbles
to my touch
effervescent
I notch each loss
deeply into
the walls
a makeshift
memorial
I long for neat
parallel lines
to honor the dead
but my hands
tremble
unsteady

Body as a Burial
Crystal Kinistino

My body is an ancient burial ground
It gets desecrated by someone else's
idea of progress.
When you enter me, you stir the dead,
the anger of a century in red
pours out in tainted rivers,
the Red River,
where the missing ones were buried,
floods over and curses any attempt
I might make to love you.
Your heart gets haunted
by something unnamed,
something buried
too deep to be translated.
Your hands are the only evidence
that I exist beyond this.
You frack me without a thought
for what you take,
but what hurts most
is what you leave behind,
was once so sacred.

Another Lonely Winter
Crystal Kinistino

I am thinking I could go anywhere,
I could go now,
turn the brass knob and step out
into the blistering night,
but I would suddenly become aware
of how my blood was not so cold
It was not meant
for the unforgiving arctic
whose winds now blow
endless lines of powder
and formulate daggers of ice
on the roof across the street,
creating cocaine crystals
as white as the skin of an anglosaxon

Instead she lies in bed,
an alabaster statue,
her love for me unconfessed,
like an egg incubating in a nest
I can see her through a crack in the
blinds, as I pull her close and absorb
the heat from her somnolent body

I am thinking I could go anywhere
I could pack a bag and disappear
and the chasm would cease in time..
love might never come,
but there's nothing to keep

As the World Burns

one from searching
For all the time we spend waiting,
we spend so much time escaping
we don't think about the body
beside us if love is vacant,
we are mere corpses
getting by on time and nocturnal urges,
nightly desires to disappear,
moments when we should stay,
moments when all that has the nerve
to travel at this hour, in this bitterness,
is the rabbit who scurries faster than the train
out of harm's way

I tuck myself in safe
I am safe
complacent as a chalice of glass

You love me
You don't

It doesn't matter
I am here with you

The seasons pass
I am thinking I could go anywhere,
else I could just sleep in your arms
sheltered from the deathly embrace
of another lonely winter.

You Won't Take Her
Matthew D. Eayre

And her little hand fit right
round my thumb, she
grabbed me
A life, brand new and how
is this more than everything
How am I now
acknowledging
I was wrong?
And the nurse says, do you
want me to change her?
And I say no, you won't take
my daughter
And she smiled and farted
and she climbed and she grew
And a lot of the time I was
growing too
With life that I see
I see this life and she has
her own mind and the
teacher said, do you want
me to change her?
And I say no, you won't take
my daughter
And she's growing and
learning
And I'm not there
And I wait to see her and I
quiet my fears

As the World Burns

Because her mind is strong
And her eyes are open
And I'm not there to know
what is being said
And my fear says, whether
or not you want, I'm going
to change her
And I say no, you won't take
my daughter
And today someone said
my daughter is black
They group her in
To nice tidy stack
They cast at her feet all the
love
That they lack
And I say no, she's not
She's not what you see

She's not what you think
She's not even me
My daughter is her own
And when she has grown
You'll see, and you'll say
We're going to change her
And I say no, you won't take
my daughter

Hydra
Rachel W. Roth

A drop of rain against the ocean's mass
Alone, it lands on the painted pavement and stains like blood
Waiting for its companion forever gone
    A soul mate, their light, life entwined with mine, with ours
It is an amputation by a corroded blade
No anesthesia. I felt all the pain and alcohol has lost its effect
I fear the day I forget

        The perfect imperfections of it all
          Now just eternal spoils
Like an aquiline nose I love to trace, I still feel the ghost of your
    bones
The flecks of your remains, I can't bear to wash it away
    Remembering when they were as clear as the ocean's blue
My memory will stew in filth forever
You've been left on the slab no different than a corpse
Rotting, as if you never existed, replaced by a rot that spreads
Wildfire that burns only sanity
        The streets went dark, the sky went red
    I prayed to the God I stopped believing in to keep us
      together
Stop our hearts at the same time, keep pulsing as one
The room has never been so loud in this forever mourning
Where there were once two is now a severed half
      Their skeletons exposed from the severed skin
I'm no Hydra of Lerna
It won't grow back.

She Doesn't Live Here Any More
Rachael Z. Ikins

An Urge To Scream

S.A. Quinox

The world spins around me in a rhythm of cosmic fear.
Time dances from one corner to the next and
whispers of an unravelling. A way of coming undone
right before my eyes yet far away from my sight,
leaving heavy footprints everywhere it lands.
Everything is madness. Everything is chaos.
My bones have never collided in tranquility,
but this time I feel myself landing into a war
that's never crossed my soul before,
and it is terrifying. It is especially now when
I ache to hold and be held with love that
the world denies me every droplet of peace.
I hear them, these silent people hiding grimace
behind their masks. If we all would be allowed to scream,
I fear, the world would never know silence again.

Chaos Theory
Crystal Kinistino

A voice never to be heard. (things absurd.) The giving up of moments into memories, the sacrifice of self into nothingness, like the self was nothing to begin with, and it wasn't, it is and it is not dependent on mood. But a mood can create & destroy. What was that they told us? First the thought, then the mood, then the action. But what if I was without thought or feeling? What if I was all id, seething along on impulse, impervious to the outcome, recklessly burning the night alive like a dying star? What if that's all we are? These cellular beams of nothing, creating self from thought & illusion. The play of existence is transitory, so we can opt to live or die, or merge into another self at random, according to our own will, that gets governed by the heart and guided by the soul, which is immortal. Then this body is a choice and so is yours but are we really free or is that also illusory? We carry our prisons like luggage or occupations, from one destination to the next, deep in our inner cores, where we fear to tread. Freedom is a state of mind they say, so I can be locked away and still fly, or I can roam forever and never feel alive. It doesn't matter either way. I dreamt we had a long conversation. I dreamt I heard your voice. I dreamt you meant to tell me something. We had met for the first time in the flesh, and there was nothing to be said that couldn't be expressed by our bodies, so you said hello with a long and fatal kiss and in that same breath I said goodbye to life and death, I was born in you, anew. Because real love makes us lose our vision and real love makes us see things as they are, in a way we were blind to before. All that pollutes us from the past transmutes into a white light of undying purity in

163

Famine

which we create each other, rhythmically like planets, aligned to a divine order, that appears to us as chaos.

martian echoes
Tony Single

this earth is a bauble turning in an echo chamber of night
and i've nothing to say that hasn't been said before
the patterns of sounds at my disposal when rearranged
become less true in words

if i'm a miracle then why am i here at all when
no pattern exists that's new and consequential
there's life on mars yet i still miss you so far away

in perpetuity i declined for my end
but now i'm grubbing out of dirt for your touch
tho' they fill my gullet with partisan stones
you make me reach for transcendence

i hope (and must) if i'm to maintain this belief that
we'll meet again beyond the art of memory
love, you will not be abandoned and forgotten
i cleave to you, we are human
and this is our story

Just Us
Matthew D. Eayre

It's just us, here, in the
space between thought
and ear, living on love and fear
It's just us and we fuss and
we fight and we're wrong
when we're right and we
can't hit the lights until the
party's over,
It's over, it's over, hit the
fucking light and let me sleep
It's just us, here, not
soldiers and kings,
Not sharp teeth or wings,
we're supposed to be the
ones that do the great
things and we are what we
eat, a life full of heat
burning meat from the
bone, we can't stop and we
can never go home, it's just
us, here
So whisper close, love,
whisper hard and true,
please don't you stop until I
know what to do, it's just
us, here
Yell, scream, just tell me
your dreams and I'll try to

As the World Burns

make sense of things in
past tense, I'll fight to get
clear what the symbols
meant, I will, just tell me,
It's just us here. We've been
here and we will but it's
only us. In a world full of
metal we write buildings to
dust and we stain into rust
with the tears we evoke,
not a metaphor, no images,
Just a noise in the smoke
It's just us here so don't
hold back, we don't have
anything else to feel,
nothing left that's real, no
pews to go pray in,
God lives where I kneel, it's just
us and it won't change
when I open my eyes, I've
seen through my lies all
along,
I didn't know the words
I have always known wrong
It's just us here
We can stumble and
fumble about, we can rage
and retire from the voices
that shout, we can and we
will be just what we are,
just you, just me
It's just us here

Holding On

A. Shea

. . . if we only held on
to life every day
like we do
when we are afraid
of losing it.

Conquest

How do we?
Jane Dougherty

How do we wake when the day is dark
as midnight ink and sea rolls and roils
thick as smoke?

Why turn and rise with the habitual gestes
when the wind yells and the trees fall
and birds tossed like paper bags
steer their chaotic way through the gloom?

It is coming the great flood
fire or water
or scorpions with lions' heads

galloping from the open hands of the great of this world
and their acolytes with the face of the man next door.

All Roads
Kristiana Reed

Dulce et Decorum Est:
Horace said it first
wandering cobbled roads
which all led to a Rome
gaudy in marble arches
and porticoes.

Owen said it second
as men choked on mustard gas
and turned belly up in the mud
towards the unrelenting sun,
the unrelenting cold,
the unrelenting guns.

And here we are again
looking at the world
as if through a glass bottomed boat;
wondering what is sweet,
what is fitting. Wondering when
our voices will be enough
for the countries we are dying in
as sea levels rise and the big men
in the skyscrapers get richer.
Is this sweet? Is this fitting?
Are these the clothes we say our goodbyes in?
Pro patria mori.
I am laced with fury.

a new abnormal
Erik Klingenberg (nightpoet)

as this new darkness
descends
like a shroud upon our lives,
the old world withers and dies
and things will never be
as they were before,
replaced by a new abnormal
no one wants or understands,
as the shadows slowly steal
away our sanity and breath,
the reality gradually dawns
upon the human race that
it shan't be that much longer
until we all sleep with death

I don't recognize this world
Rachel Tijou

A world of insular—and archaic landscape
a world where we once looked into
each other's eyes.
Do you remember?
Childhood, was it a dream?
They wired us up and tuned us into,
the depths of our fledgling ego.
Connection
a forgotten world
blinded inversion
lighting avarice.
This earth screams in despair. We are
now masked and bound by
sadistic clowns with painted smiles.
The earth crumbles with the weight of our
Greed
Engineered
Empathy
Twisted, unrecognizable.
We are the VIRUS
Conflict saturating our effort
and the oppressed cried out for help
the whipped and chained choked
'enough'

Question Authority
emje mccarty

Am I Angry?
Inspired by Rachel "Quirky" Shenk
John W. Leys

Living at the intersection
Of Delight and Delirium,
Immersed in disposable
Consumable media
Filled with bizarre images
Of singing cats shedding their skin
And Steven Moffat's fever dreams
Of Dracula,
Trying to drown out
The intense sorrow
And existential dread
Of a world draped in darkness.

I crave the release
Of the Mighty Marvel
Morphine Drip™
To numb my mind
And help me
Momentarily forget
That a continent is burning
And seas will soon be boiling
Away to nothing
As oligarchs fiddle
With themselves,
Counting their money
While Gaia flatlines
On the table

As the World Burns

(Her insurance wouldn't
Cover the cure)

I need that Disney brand dopamine
To distract from the darkness
Threatening to drag us down
To the crossroads of
Despair and Death:

Children in cages
And coffins,
Kingdoms split apart.
Glaciers melting,
Forests burning.
People dying
On minimum wage.

Identity, humanity; agency:
Denied!
Bigoted, racist,
anti-Semitic, Islamophobic,
Transphobic, homophobic,
Xenophobic domestic terrorists
Bathed in ignorance and self-righteousness,
Strings pulled by plutocrats
And war criminals
Profiteering off the proletariat's
Blood, sweat, and tears,
Knowing that the divided
Can never band together
And guillotine the rich.

Conquest

But aren't you angry?
Why waste your time?

Am I angry?

Don't mistake immersion
In immaterial flickering lights
For apathy
When it's a bid
To save my sanity!

In this capitalistic dumpster fire
I need brightly colored flashes
Of insanity and stupidity
To keep me from madness!

Am I angry?
Here's my secret:
I'm always angry.

The Optimist
Jimmi Campkin

An Invitation
Hoda

Come with me to the river of boundlessness. Drink from the nectar of the Gods and bathe in rivers of holy coding.

Stretch the sky with both hands and leap in, left thigh first and touch the bottom of nothingness.

I want to bear the weight of a thousand cherry-yellow gold chains, holding my many names and dive into the sublime. I want to see nirvana, even if it means I gotta die.
Frank Ocean was right:

You gotta fuck with me after my shift. I catch you dripping in yesterday's prophecy, handing you the throes of your sovereignty. This isn't simply a game, to me—

What we've lived for, We will finish this time around and nothing stands in the way of a WHOLE portrait, dripping in tomorrow's paint. The future is the now in a different face.

Moving in a slower pace, with deeper grace and a field to be reckoned with.

I wonder

I wonder

I wonder

As the World Burns

Will they write stories about us? Laden pages honoring our quiet grandiosity?

Will they silence us? Fill our opened lotuses with dirt? Will they try and forget us? Forage us out of their memories, though we take to the root, mold with it, wherever we land? Will they capture our late night shape shifting? Trying on different skins, each and every one of us, buzzing and illuminating to the shade of: KIN.

Patience and blessings and Handkerchief's to the ones filled with grief, the Kali Yuga is really dancing in the dusk filled sky; Many of us, ushering the end of times, trumpet, horn, confetti, welcoming it, with a smile.

Reminded when eons ago, we danced with twisted feed around fires like these, celebrating collapsing cycles because finally: we've tapped Freshwaters. Bridging the capacity to stomach miracles from the greatest architect of reality.

Say You Want a Revolution?
Katherine DeGilio

My years have gone away.
They've danced and partied against the lines on my face.
The sun was the warmth and the prey
the eager could not catch,
They stood against duality,
rather than rage against polite beasts.
Then their tear lines began to wither,
as they starved while others would feast.

Distancing against the traditional,
but holding tight to our mother's bread,
let's eat with thieves and sinners
rather than by a king be led.
Yet, no one in the -ocracy, would speak another word.
We all have our ideas of which prefix should come first.
Arist, and dem, perhaps mon if bent,
the letters wither a while.
For everyone wants the adrenaline of change
without the fear of trial.

Serendipity
Kim D. Bailey

We are dancing in our kitchen to Jimmy Hendrix's song, "Little Wing," barefoot, hair disheveled, wearing goofy grins. I am perspiring, partly from the sweltering August heat in South Central Pennsylvania, partly because I am a woman who has outlived her youth. Summers in Georgia and Florida could not prepare me for this kind of heat. Heavy. Penetrating. Steady.

So much like his eyes. He gazes into mine as we move in a small circle, embracing one another despite the warmth. The color of gunmetal blue to my brown draw me in. I touch his face, caressing his beard. He pulls me closer with his hand firmly holding me steady.

Outside the world is chaos. The news brings pain and confusion in heaping, daily doses. Hate and derision spew from the orange man who seems hell bent on destroying what is left of our democracy, sold out by the Washington elite to the highest bidder. Black people continue to push back, braver but still terrified, trying to reconcile nearly 300 years of oppression. White supremacists shed their masks, unashamed of their deeply held belief that "White is Right." We still live in a man's world, especially when the men are white, with money and power. Finally, we are six months into a pandemic. COVID-19 has altered our lives and brought a new normal of masks, hand sanitizer, social distancing, and fear that the person coughing in the next aisle at the supermarket could possibly be carrying the virus that will kill us. Our lives are uncertain at each turn.

185

Conquest

We can feel the fear and rage pulsing deep in our marrow in tune with the world's heartbeat. Humanity has found a new low. Yet, for the first time in my 53 years of life on this rock, in my small space and blip on the timeline, I feel safe. I am loved.

We laugh together, ever mindful of how lucky we are. We play the alternate realities in our minds and speak openly about serendipity. Had we not met on that dating site four months before lockdown, a mere couple of months before COVID-19 struck the first American down, we know we'd be in our old lives, boxed and barely breathing. Begging for someone to love us, to see us for who we are, chasing the next high and thrill and aware of our singular states of loneliness. Hope's flame flickered but burned hot, its blue center refused to surrender to the darkness.

We remain cognizant of the world's distress. The two of us have fought for marginalized people, defying our own families and risking alienation from the people we once believed we could depend on. Yet, we cannot long withstand the steady stream of hateful rants from the mad man in the White House, the daily reports of COVID-19 deaths and outbreaks, or another Breaking News story of a black man killed by white hands because of the color of his skin.

So, we dance here together and kiss the sorrow away. We know. The virus could take one of us tomorrow. A stray bullet or a blocked artery could find its way to one of our hearts. World or Civil War could erupt, and our lives may become nothing but a dance of survival.

As the World Burns

Meanwhile, we allow happiness to fill the darkness and shine on as we sway to the rhythm of a song.

I Know
Jaya Avendel

I know the world is burning
Because I drip sweat at midnight
And my friends do not look like friends
Behind masks splattered with
Watermelon seeds.

I know the world is burning
Because we shout from across the street
Afraid to touch
Needing to love
But the wind steals our breath away.

I know the world is burning
Because the past is an unknown planet
Undiscovered or
Forgotten.

I know the world is burning
Because the flames touch my heart and
Burn books that predicted the future
Seven dozen years ago
Before I had a choice
Before I could choose another life.

I know the world is burning
Because my human heart is consumed
Cleansed and bleached white and
It is a choice to herald change.

As the World Burns
Kindra M. Austin

My heart beats; rage
breaks against rib cage and
weeps into toes.
Shoes don't fit, and I walk bare
as the world burns my hope
into cinder.
I collect cremated dreams under my nails,
as the world burns my paper wing love.
As the world burns,
I wheeze from punctured lung.
My patience is burned to ember,
as the mother fucker burns—
fuels hate with fictions.
My heart beats, and
I recall laughter escaped from my girl's mouth.
I recount the stars in her eyes,
and my heart beats as the world burns.
I gather up dust from my hair, and spit into
my palms.
I will fashion and fire new bricks
for her,
as the world burns.

A Quiet Nihilism
Nicholas Gagnier

The world is burning, but
the fires aren't even. One cleaves through the forest,
burning burrows and branches;
another is flame over
oil floating
on water, blocking off
the spoils of war.
Another fire savages a
town of people, but because
they're second in the scheme of
citizens— those without capital or collateral—
face only unilateral decline,
while the ones
with two decent footings
standby and argue about whose inferno was worth
saving.

It wasn't the village. That couldn't be pillaged.
It wasn't the forest, because
that would be too
transformative for people who still control the
world run on the business of death,
entrepreneurs kept abreast
of the tragedies in
which they
stand to
gain
the

As the World Burns

most.
The world is burning, but there's no honest reason.
You don't have to take it from me, though. I've long given up
trying to be any semblance of a force for good. I would try
again,
but there
are
better
people than me,
they all say— those kinds of people solve the
world's problems, don't they?

I'm not altogether convinced.

Burn It Down
emje mccarty

burn it down

(senryu – "colors")
John Cochrane

As the world burns down,
Black and white and brown fight blue—
Orange's race war.

Birthing Pains

John Biscello

To see, everywhere,
brave little lights going up,
flares of hope and justice,
holding hands
to tip the scales
in a bond of solidarity,
a fire-chastened purge
and desire for change's
holy golden grail,
the quest,
a blessed rhyme
and legacy,
with each and every
one of our hearts
breaking open
to scale the ribs of light
and become radical midwives
to a collective rebirth.

The Price of Power

reflections on the mass murder in El Paso
Dustin Pickering

how do leaders inspire—
their words are breathing into our world

don't let them say what they will
or others will do what they will

the feeble and stupid emulate power
thinking themselves powerful

those with confidence and strength
are adored by weaklings and fakes

so if you want the strife and the fear
exit remorseless from our scene

Being is timeless and belongs to us all

loose
dani bowes

i cut my hair too short in quarantine
now pieces, uneven fall
when i knot my hair up high
always out of the way, like me,
saying: "is that ok?" "i'm sorry"
apologetic is honey from the hive over
a phone line but not in 2020 with headlines
stinging and leaving welts over protestors
breathing through face masks and toppling
monuments that never should've been erected,
i hold that strength in my chest, mustering courage
when i dig
through those strands and try to pin them up
but they always come loose.

Submersion
Christine E. Ray

waters rose
'round me
so gradually
so soothingly
I barely noticed
when gentle lapping
against bare toes
became insistent
nudging of knees
hips
shoulders
with a feeling
that could be described
relief
I let it gently close
over my head
abandoning myself
to bob
sway
boneless
beneath the surface
from time to time
angel fish
whisper to me
resist
resist
I fight to emerge
filling lungs

Conquest

painful gasp
after painful gasp
with undiluted broadcasts
eyes assaulted by
unfiltered headlines
ears tormented
by buzz of a million
angry hornets
it does not
take very long
until I again
embrace surrender
drift back into
watery depths
unexpectedly grateful
to find gills
have grown
along my ribs
brightly colored fish
who do not
know the world
of men
entwined in my
seaweed hair
who dart
who play

The iPhone Morning News
Monday, August 17, 2020
Lola White

CNN

US intelligence indicates
Iran paid bounties
to Taliban fighters
for targeting US troops
in Afghanistan.

CALENDAR

Jamie's b'day
tomorrow.

THE WASHINGTON POST

Trump administration
finalizes plans
to open up
Arctic National Wildlife Refuge
to drilling.

ME

The news isn't always
listed in order of
importance.
Calendar should
come first.

Online
Nayana Nair

new list of corona jokes
new designs for mask
search: "death toll corona"
zoom
cleaner, quieter world
animals on street
search: "death toll corona"
fake rumours, fake remedies
mass graves in italy
delete: "fwd-the truth behind corona - conspiracy"
i can't breathe
retweet, retweet, retweet,
retweet, blm, retweet
40 freshest corona jokes (updated)
zoom updates, meetings
power failures, new found panic
difficult lives of doctors
essential workers
30 hilarious essential worker memes
search: "?"
search: "death toll corona"
search: "lockdown india"
search: "online stores, grocery shopping"
quarantine special youtube
police brutaility, blm, retweet, retweet,
retweet, retweet, retweet, donate,
celebrities at marches, retweet,
search: "death toll corona"

As the World Burns

homemade santizers

ignore: "hobbies in quarantine"

ignore: "sites to help you through quarantine"

ignore: "not so subtle bullying for the sake of protests - open
   your purses"

ignore: "am i still not done with falling out of love?"

blm poems

blm articles

blm newsletter

the voices that are easy to hear, because it is good business
now

pros of capitalism

tips from hong kong protesters flooding timelines

retweet, retweet, retweet, retweet

ignore: "the numbing heart- side-effect of being overwhelmed"

search: "death toll corona"

search: "death toll corona india"

lockdown extended

ignore: "half year that flew by"

ignore: "the cultivation of toxicity by my dear family"

search: "how to sleep better"

search: "new movies to watch"

search: "suicide of bollywood actor"

search: "nepotism"

ignore: "corona cases - india on #3"

ignore: "failing measures to contain pandemic"

ignore: "death toll corona"

ignore: "death"

retweet

virus
Erik Klingenberg (nightpoet)

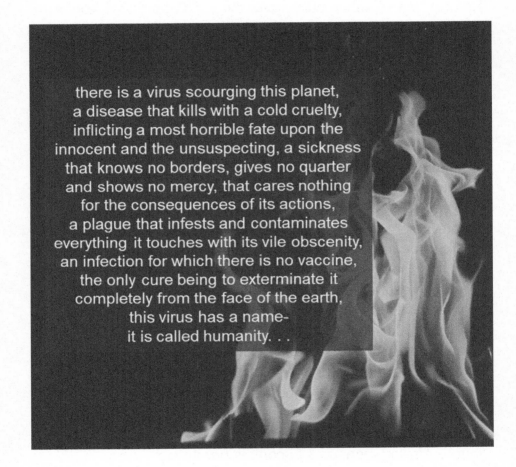

there is a virus scourging this planet,
a disease that kills with a cold cruelty,
inflicting a most horrible fate upon the
innocent and the unsuspecting, a sickness
that knows no borders, gives no quarter
and shows no mercy, that cares nothing
for the consequences of its actions,
a plague that infests and contaminates
everything it touches with its vile obscenity,
an infection for which there is no vaccine,
the only cure being to exterminate it
completely from the face of the earth,
this virus has a name-
it is called humanity. . .

Summer at the South Pole

Sally Zakariya

> *A heat wave in Antarctica melted 20% of an*
> *island's snow in 9 days. —CNN, 2/24/20*

64.9 degrees in Antarctica
it's summer down south
no swimsuits
no suntan lotion
no beach umbrellas
not yet

4 inches of snowpack
on one island thaws
in just a week

an iceberg the size
of Seattle breaks away
from Mother Ice
not overnight
but gone

polar home of 9
out of every 10 gallons
of our fresh water
melting away

highest contributor
to sea level rise
this summer

meanwhile
penguins practice
sun bathing

Something's Burning, a Pantoum in Three Parts
Carol H. Jewell

I.

With the slow smokeless burning of decay
or covered with mud after heavy rain and deforestation,
the hillsides looked as sad as hillsides could,
while activists of every stripe held their signs, in a diverse
    crowd.

Mudslides from heavy rain deforestation
caused loss of flora and fauna
while activists of every stripe held their signs, in a diverse
    crowd
and tried to embrace and avoid each other, at the same time.

The loss of flora and fauna has happened
since the world began, but never so quickly as now.
The people tried to embrace and avoid each other, at once,
as bewildered children tried to make sense of it all.

Since the beginning of time, but never so quickly
has the loss of our world been followed so slowly by rebirth.
The children are confused and cry, seeing
our swamp of a world, now drowned, now frozen.

Loss should be followed by rebirth, but faster.
Too late, cried the mourning crowd for the cause, who tried so
    hard
to warm the frozen swamp as best it could
with the slow smokeless burning of decay.

As the World Burns

II.

The loss of flora and fauna has happened
since the world began, but never so quickly as now.
The people tried to embrace and avoid each other, at once,
as bewildered children tried to make sense of it all.

Since the world began, people have tried to change it.
They cut down trees and put up buildings,
as bewildered children try to make sense of it all,
but nothing makes sense anymore.

The men cut down trees and put up buildings
and congratulated each other, and watched buildings fall
in a world that no longer makes sense
because, still, nothing can stop the earthquakes.

The men patted each other on the back, then
lounged around with their fancy cigars,
because nothing can stop the earthquakes,
and insurance will cover everything, anyway.

Sitting around, puffing away,
trying to embrace and avoid each other at once.
Insurance will take care of their real estate
but nothing will cover the loss of flora and fauna.

Conquest

III.

The men cut down trees and put up buildings
and congratulated each other, and watched buildings fall
in a world that no longer made sense
because, still, nothing can stop the earthquakes.

"Good job, old man!" Still they watched the buildings fall,
and they watched people crying over police brutality,
and knew that nothing could stop those earthquakes,
unless the people really came together against The Man.

Police brutality, deforestation, fracking.
It seems whatever The Man wants, The Man gets.
Unless the people really come together against The Man,
the world will burn and freeze and burn. And burn.

Whatever The Man wants, The Man gets
until the crowd overpowers The Man,
not in a cycle of burn and freeze, and burn,
but in one of love and compassion.

Until the people overpower The Man
in a world that no longer makes sense,
only then, in a world of love and compassion
will men tear down buildings and plant new trees.

Mother Gaia is on fire
Melita White

Mother Gaia is on fire
In her womb it burns and twists
Her flood of blood our exit wound
We are haemorrhaging
Caia Caecilia, goddess of fire
Protector of women
And hearth of home, container of fire
(Element of Gaia)
Save us all by shrinking flames
Create a heart(h) for our home
Our Mother Gaia
Contain the flames
But let the fire fuel our fight
Let it stay in our hearts
But not destroy us
Our anger's bright
Our anger's the thing that fuels the fight

While Gaia twists in uterine torsion
The head of her baby is squashed and dead
The brains of our leaders no longer work
They protect the tumour instead of the source
High ranking socios, psychos and pimps
They dance with the devil
In the dark of the shadows
Strangers to light they wander blind
Like moles out of tunnels
Can't see what's right

Conquest

Let's cauterise capitalism
It's a cancer that feeds misogyny
It feeds the greed of entitled scum
Devoid of love and of all empathy
Rewarding themselves with trophy wives
While the (m)otherness of our landscape dies
Mother Gaia is a m(other)
She's a woman and she's on fire
Burn the witch at the stake
We don't need women
Unless they bear us strong boy children
To make us more money
To swell our egos and hubris and wealth
Keep the factories going
Where the other works
Where the other bleeds
Is enslaved and tortured
To feed the greed
Of the fat white slug called misogyny

While Gaia burns and the people flee
Thousands run for the water
Red wash fills the sky
Armageddon is here
Stop the fucking lies
We can see with our eyes
That the day has come
To overthrow scum—
Let's cut out the tumour
And save our home

P is for Pangolin
Henri Bensussen

cuddly wrap of animal that's treated
as specialty. In some parts of Asia
a delicate delicacy, bush meat in Africa.
Pangolin only wants to scoop up ants
or termites, protected from bites by its
scales, used as medicine* for those
who can afford it. P is for Payment.

A treasure of mammalian affection
if approached with care and love. Like
women. When under attack curls itself
into a scaly snail of a ball, impossibly
impenetrable, unlike women. P is for
Patriarchy, porn, pimp, power, power-
less, poverty, pride and Primate.

Which is us, taking over the world,
eating it up, consuming because we can.
P is for pest and pester, perverse and pervert
penetrate and pillage, you get the picture
as does the pangolin, caught in traps
hunted, enslaved, auctioned, or butchered:
P is for Price, the Market, Stock Exchange

And all the other ways we pay for what
we call freedom. P is for privilege, pleasure,
and pleas for mercy, for passion and purpose,
pawn, passport, peace, peril, and the pickle
we're in over perversity of impulse. P is for
the propensity to act without Prudence.

*Ancient Chinese medicine postulates that "the distinctive scales [of the Pangolin]
embody both Penetration and Protection. From this, the open-ended Powers to
Penetrate blockages within the body, and to give Protection, are
deduced." (Wikipedia)

Southern Crows
Hokis

A single bat escaped the Amazon fires
reached the Wuhan market
to hunt and gather food for her refugee family.

This is where we mark the beginning
explain why our cars cower from nature's cycle
retreat into caves as dusk's crows quietly perch
along backyard branches and electrical wires
filling the canopy of our neighborhoods.

Here in the arboretum where I walk my dogs
gravity pulls at the souls of my feet
each thump of my boot leaves the imprint of my elders
land and life forms who instructed my childself
to listen to the lack of noise created by that darkest crow.

Flashes of my grandfather's farm
the open-to-the-cosmos skies
soy fields would yield to the rain's promise
form a banked home for predators and prey alike
there I would sit, atop a blanket so the biting chiggers couldn't
    nip.

This image as vivid as the contract written
for nature's love song band;
bullfrog's belching bass line
cricket's steady unrelenting heartbeat chorus
volume raising with heat, softening with cold

As the World Burns

always swooned were the nested lovers whose ears were
    tuned
those fireflies at the bar, flashing above the scum
causing Light's predators to pause, clear space.

The truth in that tick-tock
the life and death of the dark-lit moon sky
the silence in the nipless noise
I shudder from the beauty
then shine in that memory of the
streetlightless playground I called Home.

The morning after came in blaring, waking the cow.
the sweetest mooing and cooing to greet my ears
the chewing of cud at my window
our dark brown eyes meet

a hushing pain of glass between us
we gaze into each other, as a nod
we know their pies remain
uselessly baking in today's sun.

These vigilant senses never pass
today those lessons bite my visions
call me to turn towards the sound of this moment's silence.
Today I realize the black birds resting are not southern crows
but those righteous bats whispering
"Are they all dead yet?"

Grow
A. Shea

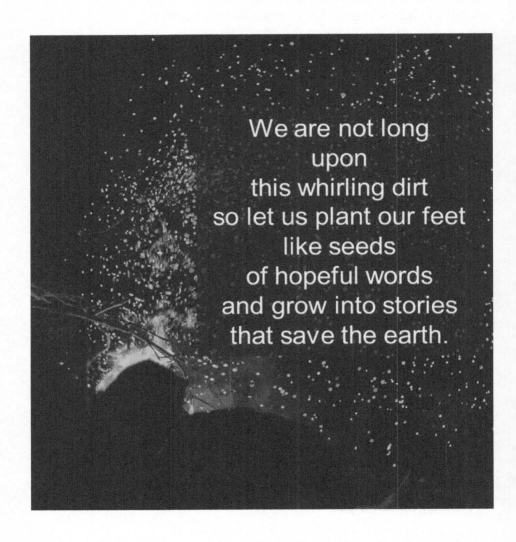

We are not long
upon
this whirling dirt
so let us plant our feet
like seeds
of hopeful words
and grow into stories
that save the earth.

Red
Patricia Q. Bidar

We Americans reside in a time when our every action carries a shadow: how much does this matter if the minute hand edges closer to permanent midnight? Does anything matter?

And yet the signs of nature are here for us to see, and smell, and hear. The uncanny yellow of daffodils, the trill of birdsong, clouds drifting across powdery skies. Our jacaranda's canopy turning sparse, as it always does in the weeks before the heavenly blooms billow forth.

Today, because of a freelance writing job, I learned that Pentecost is sometimes known as the birthday of the church. Pentecost Sunday is a day to mark the presence of the Holy Spirit with the earliest Christians as they gathered after Jesus' death. This was 50 days after Easter. ("He is risen!")

My knowledge of these things is spotty. But I love Jesus. The Jesus Christ, Superstar Jesus. Jesus of the gospels, bountiful hang time with misfits and hoes, and flowing Dan Fogelberg hair. That Jesus is just all right with me; all right, oh yeah.

"I believe in the golden rule. Whoever has the gold makes the rules" was stenciled on a sign in our grandfather's home bar. He also had an oil painting of a sexy female toreador wearing only stiletto heels, brandishing a pair of red panties at a bull. One time, he told us our grandmother was the model. (Another time, he said he himself was the model for the profile on the head of the American dime.)

Conquest

Behind the bar as our parents and grandparents played poker in the next room, my sister and I would loll, eating maraschino cherries and ruining the bright paper drink parasols to inspect the tiny strips of Chinese newspaper inside.

So, I didn't have a religious upbringing. And it was for the first time today that I learned that "we" mark Pentecost Sunday with the color red. See, on that first Pentecost Sunday, people were on fire with the Spirit, loving and praising God.

Red is the color of exposed skin, strange words issuing forth, the believers gleefully rowing, posing on precipices, or dancing badly under the trees. I see snakes dangling down, hissing out sales pitches to sunburnt ears.

That fire is not red, but orange. And I will forever associate with that spiteful hue the shadow civilization that has exposed itself in my country like an ancient tree's wet, rotten roots.

Tonight, at the confluence
Sarah Bigham

You speak of bells and thundered paws
Those tongues they fly but free
For now the time has come for them
—no celebrations of the soul—
When you shed those long blazed tears
While raging before the hired guns
Within a night of deepest blue
There once were shells beneath your feet
But now the churning turns toward land

The Midnight Sun
Sun Hesper Jansen

I have painted, since I can remember, this melting sun,
and in every ray of bleeding oil is a face no one recalls
but me. You're making this worse, you say; you wish
I would stop, paint something/anything new, to paint
you, as if love will keep the earth from incineration.

The power you give me, when I only paint what we
have made, and I'm sorry that the burning cities on my
canvases give no relief, and in the shadows, blood pools
and glaciers melt and myriad species add their bones to
the fossil record, but I can do anything now but stop.

Because nothing has felt real for so long, you believe
we inhabit The Twilight Zone. That all I need to do to
cool the world, and your frantic heart under my cheek,
is paint a waterfall. Fall asleep and dream this a fever,
with cool peace and reason waiting on the other side.

In November, you say, we'll wake up to a different
world. But I know my Rod Serling, and in that world
the sun's been left behind, and cool, silencing snow
falls soft as complicity, freezing blood, growing glaciers
over the fossil record as we race into endless night.

I can do anything now but stop.

And you can do anything but sleep.

So wake with me, and work.

A memo to those in power
Erin Van Vuren

Oh, how your
kingdom will
fall...
When you find
that your
discarded pawn
was the queen
all along.

– Erin
Van Vuren

@papercrumbs

The Very, Very Un-President
Tremaine L. Loadholt

he builds sandcastles of
lies houses his men of
fury,
whines when the way isn't
his, and boosts hatred
higher on its pedestal.

a misogynistic micro-
aggressor branded in
narcissism, his will isn't the
way.
the blind is leading the blind
and those of us with third
eyes have them wide open.

we see everything.

Nasty, Consecrated
Marcia J. Weber

brand me nasty
    dost thou?
flailing irons white
hot with ire
fanned in the orang-ed
    inferno
of your raging
impotence

                I own your epithet
               rooted, as it were
         in your dread
                    of my
                 unassailable
                 articulation
        of truths

your words
    incoherent babbles
founder as you flounder
grasping - desperate -
for poison-arrowed straws
    vicious gasping
stock in trade
of the school yard bully

Conquest

                                        should I cower?
                                        mask my womanhood
                        lest you grab
                                        assault - your blanket -
                                        protection against
                        vociferous protestations

tattoo your taunts
        panicked projectiles
bold upon my breast
bared in sisterly solidarity
inoculations inked
        arms linked
poised in the face
of your dastardly fabrications
                                        no verecund damsel here
                                        cogent arguments to hand
                        I persist
                                        the distilled venom of your hate
                                        leaks from your member
                        limp in your frantic hands

As the World Burns

is this what you wanted (apologies to leonard)
Tony Single

i went walking in the midst of loud appeals
to the better drone of my nature
and forcefed promises to be made anew
in a yonder framed for the chosen few

who'd have known what the future would hold
been naïve enough to believe again
what once was a cradled, spotless bloom
now a weight of years fills that foom

trump still lives, yet cohen's dead
fascism's risen, your god is bled
now peel back my skin and bruise me within, why don't ya
trump still lives, yet carrie's dead
iceland's too warm and the oceans are red
now peel back my skin and rub the salt in, hallelujah

the diamonds got all unearthed down here
the stars up there all got pretty scanty
was god just a man with a beard and a view
where did the dinosaurs all vanish to

yeah, something about this rain makes me heavy
i'll weep from pustules 'til i grieve no more
my bottle cradled, one more nuclear bloom
now a weight of bones fills the foom

Conquest

trump still lives, yet marilyn's dead
your food is porn, greed gives more head
now peel back my skin to the china within, why don't ya
trump still lives, yet bowie's dead
the bees are all gone and the birds have fled
now peel back my skin and tilt the gin in, hallelujah

Orange
Carrie L. Weis

Orange used to be full of sugar-coated jelly slices.
It was the miniature glass of juice
set at the upper right hand
with just a breadth of space between it and the plate
before even breakfast arrived on the table.
Proclaiming the juice were as much
a part of the place setting as forks and knives.

Orange was the color of pumpkins filled with promises of candy
and flickering candles,
of toothy grins carved into soft flesh.
Orange represented the most important color
on the Candy Corn triad,
weighting the bottom,
providing ballast,
so there was never an argument over top and bottom.
Up and down.

Orange was the color of Key West sunsets
while lovers held hands
kissing the sun farewell
and bidding the last breath of day adieu.
The kisses like those planted on rosy cheeks
of babes at bedtime.
Knowing suns and children rise each morning
but never to the same moment in time.
The world moves on.

Conquest

Orange was a color on the spectrum
perfectly aligned between yellow and red
before
the world twisted off its axis,
slid slightly towards the abyss,
and turned around a different sun.
A different bloated orange body
whose light
really does not shine
whose heat
cannot warm its own core.
Orange is now a stain that will never be released
From the fabric of your favorite silk shirt.

"Orange is like a man, convinced of his own powers."
Wassily Kandinsky

There Was More Than One Wall
Katherine DeGilio

The orange man promises a wall.
He yells that it will come soon.
I look at my father,
his conservative brow knits as he looks at my colors.
I open my mouth to speak but shut it.
The orange man promises a wall.
My words leave frown lines on my father's forehead.
The word impeachment burns on the screen,
A commentator wonders
if the orange man will keep his commitments.
I reach out for republican hands,
and they pull away, as if I am a viper.
The orange man promises a wall,
but there's already so many.

Comeuppance
with Mullen and Limón

Kim Harvey

just as I am I come
—H.M.

a wild beast's fur I come
come fox come wolf come
fortunate one why these blues
come from us   we all come
from   doldrums   did he come
sober did he cover her mouth
in a manner unbecoming
to justice did he come in first
come first served   did he refuse
to come clean scrub this bum star
collide with truth collude some
news   fake muse   lemon come
melon come   melania come
on   just us girls here in the room
income   outcome   how come
come close closer come here come
home   say tomorrow doesn't
come on down the price is gold comb-
over don't wear out your welcome
mat   honeycomb cereal   come
here honey   surreal I am am I come
back to the coop you flew summa
cum dotcom romcom dog is gonna
have his day in court all kingdoms come

As the World Burns

to an end   even this one   and come
november remember remember   the fox
is loose and chickens will come home
to roost off with their heads all the king's
horses pony up y'all even kumquats
can make a comeback but oranges aren't
the only fruit   come often come
early the ice man cometh give 'em
their due they won't see this coming
I promise you come out come out
wherever you are change is gonna come

Previously published by Poets Reading the News

Current Events
Marvlyn C. Vincent

We say, "Black lives matter,"
They say, "All lives matter."
We say, "Global warming is happening,"
They ask, "What world are you living in? Global warming isn't
even a thing."
We say, "God help us! For you know that man in the oval, and
you know he's dangerous."
They say, "He is our savior, God sent him to save us."
With that belief, it appears
like we're living in a parallel universe.
Daily, we see people marching the streets,
black parents are restless, at night they can't sleep.
Their kids are slaughtered,
and what's even worse, is that it's legally ordered.
Documents may not directly say "Kill them,"
but explain to me, what does this mean,
"Bring law and order by any means necessary?"
Cops read that as a free pass,
shoot first then ask questions last.
Blacks are killed in their sleep or walking the street,
being black it does not matter,
and with this President , it'll only get harder.
If you follow the news, you know his only concern is, his high
ratings, and his base views.
The number of Americans homeless, it's disheartening.
But that's not his business, it doesn't bother him.
He and his family are together, and they're living the dream.
While from their parents, kids are separated,

As the World Burns

his excuse, this lawlessness and illegal activities,
in our country; they are no longer tolerated.
But then in this country, kids are hungry,
Dads are innocently, incarcerated.
Single moms fighting to make ends meet,
selling their bodies, so the kids can eat.
Now this may not all be new,
it's been happening for decades,
from the moment the natives had to suffer from the white man's
raids.
Reading real history, yes, it's heartbreaking,
but admit it, we never imagined even with abolishment, it'd be
this bad.
Now, we see it has been lying dormant,
waiting for someone to proclaim himself a worthy opponent.
And at last he has,
been given power,
left and right, signing Executive order,
thumping his chest, "I'm here, to bring law and order,"
"To make America great again."
No,
you're not,
because of you, this nation's writhing in pain.
We're separated,
blacks and whites no longer integrated.
With him at the helm, this nightmare will never end.
The only way forward is to abandon this coward.
This nation needs unity,
not just between blacks and whites,
but for every community.
Sexuality's being attacked,
if you're of the LGBT++ community,

Conquest

using their bibles,
they will claw at your dignity, question your humanity.
A belief that starts from the top, embraced by Christianity,
endorsed by the president and his VP.
Certain communities being stripped of their identities.
Trans are killed after suffering atrocities.
If he's re-elected,
four years on, where will we all be?
I'm asking for real, this is not rhetorical,
cause if another four years he's made to repeat,
may heavens help us, cause we're heading up sh*t's creek.

Scarecrow Calls Out the Man
Robert Okaji

These things I cannot name: that finger of night
between fear and peace, in which darkness both cloaks
and hugs the wide-eyed. A snake, in the open. And that space
behind the watcher? Perhaps it is easier to call it something
else - a gasp, or the immeasurable measure. A presidential
folly. My friends, ever cautious, swoop in and away, taking
with them only those grains they need, unlike you. What use
is a hoarded larder if it rots? How does one come to want
everything and nothing at the same time? A gilded house
spotlights wealth, not right. Is this edifice your legacy,
your monument to self? The ventilator's whoosh paints one
forever, your pursed lips, another. But even the bunker
you cringe in lacks permanency; regard your hands
and all they can't stuff into your pockets. Loosen that
coiled tie lest it choke you. Accept what the mirror sees,
and await karma. Though you will not hear my voice,
I offer this: may the combined weight of your lies and
larcenies, your unpaid debts and power plays, rapes,
casual racism, privilege and coarse, childish taunts, merge
into one fist-size bankroll placed upon your chest, and
fueled by the gravitational forces of forty-four black holes,
slowly, with each turn of the earth's axis, press down and
down and down in search of that shriveled organ, and finding
it, pluck out and replace it with one resembling that of a
genuine human, one honoring respect and love, empathy
and humility. I am the sum of integrated, discarded
pieces assembled to observe and warn, collecting only
diminishment and the means to become less. Wanting

Conquest

little, the world welcomes me. It arrives free, honest, on
wings, bringing wealth beyond your reach, your greed.
I own nothing. I know nothing. But this: I name you
Scourge, and laugh at the smallness of you. I name you
Farce. I name you Empty. I name you Gone.

"Scarecrow Calls Out the Man" was originally published in *Vox Populi*, August 2017.

As the World Burns

President
Izabell Jöraas Skoogh

Dear President,

I am

praying that your intentions
are not as unpleasant as your words.
The words are spilling out of your mouth
when your jaw starts moving. I am

not scared of you,
rather worried about the signals
you exude, fearing
this world getting even darker. I am

afraid it is getting nastier than it already is.
Disliking your eager of "mine", the too much "I's"
with no sympathy whatsoever for others.
Continuing statement after statement. I am

disappointed.

Statements promising about the Straight White Man's power.
Make America great again
When was America ever great for anyone else except the
White Straight Man? I am

Conquest

wondering if you are scared Mr. President
For the minorities to feel like a part of the bigger whole.
(LGBTQ, Socioeconomic status, skin color)
You can't check the box. I am

wondering if you are scared Mr. President.
Afraid that when people are no longer helpless,
when they do not need to be spending all
their energy on surviving; they will fight you. I am

wondering if you are threatened
that your power
could be lost, Dear
White man. I am

convinced that together we will be greater
but instead of leading by example
you talk about a physical wall defining the
"I's" and "You's". I am

wondering if you are afraid to show some solidarity
Mr. President, tell me, are you?

The Intemperate Language Of Bull Tweet
Sarah Ito

Bull tweet speaks
In tongues,
The language of confusion
Draped in white sheets of alternate truth
Vague yet certain,
Like the target viewed
Through the steely sights
Of a wounded sniper
In the fog of war

Bull tweet flies
In the face of the probable,
On the wings of imaginary angels
And dies in the depths of despair
Over a cup of tea
Served with honey and blood
On a market day
In Aleppo

Bull tweet worships
At the altars of the Alt
Right and Left,
Quoting the Bible
Waving the Quran
Debating the Constitution,
And the recipe to bake
That perfect wall
Served with rice, beans, moral indignation

Conquest

And razor wire

Bull tweet dresses
To kill,
Deceptive, seductive,
Over the top and under the radar
Defying gravity
Garbed in a robe, a gown, a starched collar,
A pinstriped suit,
The tattered uniforms of a hundred nations
Blonde, blue-eyed
Dark and handsome
Kissed by lips blotted
With deadly shades
Of fake news
And stopped presses

Bull tweet speaks
In tongues,
The language of confusion
Amplified
By those who choose silence
As their weapon of choice
Others, screaming proxies for their
Unseen gods
Justified by tilted idolatry
And directionless maps,
March backwards
Until the fractious horizon
Disappears...
Two hundred and eighty characters tumble over
The slippery edge

As the World Burns

Where dead truths, like dead soldiers,
Molder in linear repose,
Forever lost in translation.

Anchor
Tia M. Hudson

America listens to yet another lie
The ground shifts, I stumble.
Weary at night, I turn, I turn back, I curse.

The warm dog curled up against
my thigh, tight and solid pressing close—
here is one true thing

The ground settles, I stand steady
The lies buzz bluebottle flies
I trap in the window.

I close them in between
screen and pane, leave them there
to die.

I run my hand one time
over the dog's back
I fall asleep on solid ground.

New Normal My Ass

emje mccarty

Generational Abuse
Maria Gianna Iannucci

he lowered his mask
and took a drag
i held my breath
as i passed
unmasked
the truth i learned to hide
is tied
to someone else's lie

Shame On Us
Susi Bocks

the greatest stories
ever told are the deceptions
given in bland kisses
by the wretched liars

there's no care
there's no real love
there's just an agenda
theirs comes first

what's at stake
is what they get from you
furthering their goals
gets them one step closer

what's at stake
is what you give them
being taken for granted
loses you your soul

War

You Should Be Angry
*In Response to the Murders of Ahmaud Arbery, Breonna Taylor,
George Floyd, David McAtee, and Tony McDade*
Teresa T. Chappell

Bite the hand that feeds you:
smear crushed chokecherries across
your cheeks, turn to the sky,
conjure storm clouds and roar
a battle cry.

Jab your finger
with a needle, let the blood
spill over the map of your being,
and stain the dirt where he
is buried, where she is buried, where
he is buried, where he is buried,
where they are buried.

Let your blood soak
the soil of unmarked graves—
in recognition of lives whose names
have been erased by a White Man's history—
my history. And if you hear voices,
good. Listen.

Deportation
Tia M. Hudson

It is my story
Those children are me

I'm a border child
  first generation here from there
What can I do, what do I do?
Those children are me

> Children cry, that's what they do
> They break the law, they pay the price
> It's a just punishment; they deserve it
> The children will be better off

I am a border child
Loving family sacrificed all
I am a teacher of others' children
Still—
Those children are me

> I never recover from the pain of loss
> I never am whole again
> Even when my mother holds me
> I know, I know
> she can be forced to let me go

Those children are me
I am a border child
What do I do now?

Borderland
Sally Zakariya

Behind a fence
across a river
wrong side of a line

The coyotes have all the cash
the agents have all the guns

Sun-scorched, bone-dry
the desert takes some souls
detention takes others

Families fractured
children in cages
and me smug-safe in the shade
of my Anglo family tree

Chop the tree down
rip up the roots
build a house of welcome
with the wood

imagine all the people
Aviva Lilith

imagine them in cars,
hondas or chevys

imagine them in bars,
vodka or bourbon.

imagine them driving to work,
thinking about being late, depressed, or scared,

imagine them in their sunday best,
imagine them at their monday worst.

imagine them making mosaics
with their childhood friends.

imagine them with their grandmothers,
learning to cook.

imagine all the people,
and the courage it took.

imagine all the people
from the far away lands,

imagine their eyes,
imagine their hands.

As the World Burns

imagine the freckle on
one of their knees,
imagine an officer
jingling keys.

imagine the power,
like frost on eyelashes.

imagine the fear,
imprisoned by fascists,

imagine all the people,
just trying to get by,
imagine all the people,
terrified they'll die.

I am An immigrant

Jesica Nodarse

Born in a land that did not recognize my human rights,
my parents risked it all to give me a better life
I am an immigrant
A piece of me will always remain in the sands of my birth
    place,
yet I have grown roots and given birth to children that proudly
    call themselves American
I am an immigrant
Forced to learn new ways
Misunderstood and misplaced
Mocked when my accent gives me away
I am an immigrant
Who fell in love with the land of the free
Who's eyes mist as our flag waves proudly
I am an immigrant
I mean you no harm
If the world were a better place I would have never left my
    home land
I am an immigrant
But that is simply a status
It says nothing of who I am
Where I've been
What I have accomplished
I am an immigrant
And if that is all you see
The problem rests with you
Not within me

Untitled
Devereaux Frazier

The day they let us go
I remember the tears
Pressing hard against my eye
A Calvary waiting to be unleashed
I watched manager Mikko announce the news
They jumped in the air, shouting in joy
I shrunk back to my locker, sat on a bench
My hands, cracked from warehouse duties
I was lucky to finally be sitting
But how long would they leave me
Sitting, waiting
Just like those bus stop corners I handled as a kid
Eyes darting for good news, fist balled for the bad
I write ballads for the bullied
And I'd pay to see your bullies frown
While I'm sitting, my head's departed
Found a suitcase and a trunk
Headed to the North Pole on a bullet train
Speeding around the world without a care for sleep
History lessons of old take center stage
Assassinations, treaties, and covert operations
Somehow they're all the same
I stay awake while I'm sitting
Mask off, because I need every single breath
The enemy hurls his tear gas and bullets
Brandishing metallic black weaponry, he's a monster
Fucking furious in frantic and unconscious berating
Truly misguided and comically adorned

War

Shielded from head to toe, ready to punish the pure
Are you truly afraid of a 5'11 guy?
With barely enough muscle to threaten a mouse
And even when it's on, do you honestly think
You'll ever stifle the assault rifle precision of a poet's mind?
I stand in the school yard, I stand among the children
Hand the grenades of truth, show the true meaning of power
Wield the cosmic deity of Love and watch thy enemies fall
This isn't a scene, no!
It's a mothafucking arms race, and my darlings
YDNAS
You don't need a silencer, not when we pour out the bowls of
    truth
Laying waste to the Facebook scientists and that one guy
Who keeps saying the country is doing great
You know whom I'm talking about
But while we're rioting, looting, sharpshooting citizens
We're so steadfast in fighting the system
That we're funding it evermore
And all the lives saved here
Still pale in comparison
To the landslide of innocent victims
Carl Gauss would be ashamed to count
The first time I looked upon a body
Dismembered and discarded
Rugged concrete with bloody mortar shards
Strewn about him in a deserted city street
Draperies hung torn and disorganized
From windows that became sniper's nest
Once home to a family, now a kill house
Heavy boots and armored trucks roar past
Cultural landmarks and sacred places

As the World Burns

Emptied of body and soul in the light
A thousand missiles transform silence
Into a cacophony of screams and terror
It appears a sacrifice has been made
A trade under the table, away from sight
The sanctity of freedom pushed
To the center of the table
With eyes on two hundred million barrels
Waiting, with seductive gaze at each player
My reader
Look at what has become of our world
Where history is forgotten and the people
Scarcely attended to and left to fade
Like an old home, trashed and rent
A child's tears are worth more than gold
Yet they work hundreds of hours
To put lining in our smartphones and TVs
I ask my friends where will they go
But the crow outside the window
Seems far more interesting
Than the lonely eyes that gaze into my soul
When I travel, when I read
Help me; you've ensnared us with ignorance
Free us now, or free us never
Just open eyes and see
You will not know our pain anymore

Blackout Art I

D. M. Burton

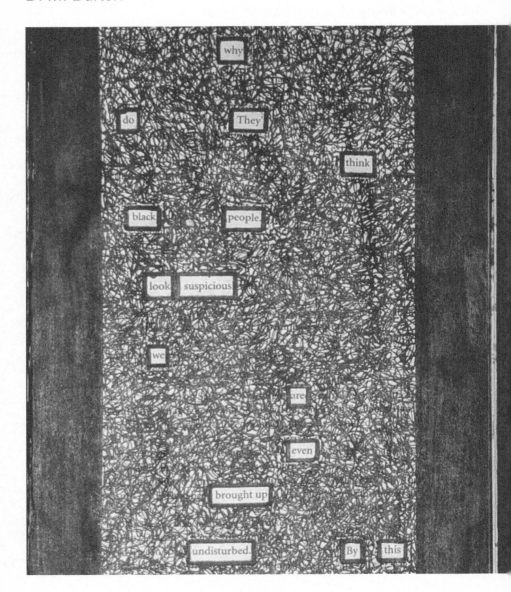

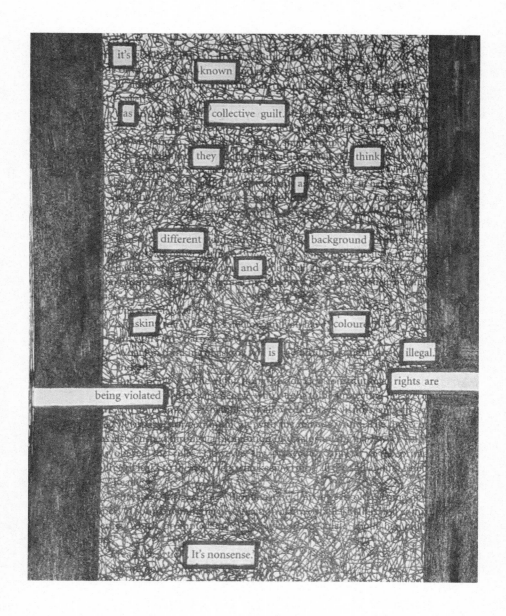

Hazard
Melissa Fadul

Because my students wear hoodies
in the rain. Because they leave their houses for 7- Eleven
pursuing *Skittles* and iced tea cravings.
Because a cop threw Andrew against a brick wall
because he fit a suspect's description.
Because it could have been Arnold who is on a full ride to
    college,
hit with a bullet in the stomach while swallowing rainbow
    candies—
Because I could see Mike sprint away because he's scared
someone is following him—not because he did anything.
It could have been his blood running down a sewer drain,
mixing with *Skittles* dye—his candy and corpse
covered with sand after the body was pronounced dead.
It could have been Ron, who asked me before the Ferguson
    riots,
Why do blacks still sit in the back of the bus
if they don't have to anymore?
I asked him, *do you?*
He just looked down at his desk.
Because Keith told me and only me why Joel was in bed under
    the covers all week—
Monday, after practice, we jumped a subway turnstile and a
    cop pulled a gun on us.
Because the other day, my oldest friend's husband, Derek
    repeated,
that could've been me just taking a jog—I could've have been
    shot.
Are you scared

As the World Burns

to go for a run now? I asked him.
Not in New York where we live—other places, yes. He
answered.
My wife is from Kentucky, while it's not the same,
there are counties like Hazard,
we couldn't even hold hands
or order a wedding cake. I added.
Prejudice is prejudice, he responded.
In the background, my oldest friend, Nicole yells, *white*
    privilege.
A week later, a witness records an officer kneeling
on the neck of a black man
lying on his stomach for almost nine minutes
before an ambulance came.
I hope I would have been the one to jump on top of the cop.
Because it could have been Derek—
because it could have been
me at his funeral
with my arms around Nicole
trying to hug the hurt out of her.

Poet Conjures
Tamara J. Madison

"In 38 minutes of fear and chaos today, an unarmed woman with a history of mental illness lead secret service and law enforcement on a wild car chase. After ramming into the barricade next to the White House and later circling the peace monument, she was fatally shot without leaving her driver's seat; the one-year old infant in the back seat survived. A moment of silent prayer was held on the House floor for the officers injured who feared for their lives and the safety of others.

In other news, God committed suicide, his body found dangling on a teepeed tree rooted in the White House lawn. The locals surmised a lynching. Their suspicions remain unmerited."

> While others fuel the frenzy,
> fodder for another kill,
> I bless and wash the feet of Time.
> Holy water dripping from my palms,
> I carefully collect broken souls,
> enough to plant a garden,
> from the bloodied soil,
> sculpt a woman.
> Between mantra, mojo, conjure,
> soon be over this mourning.

The Lungs of Oppression
Selene Crosier

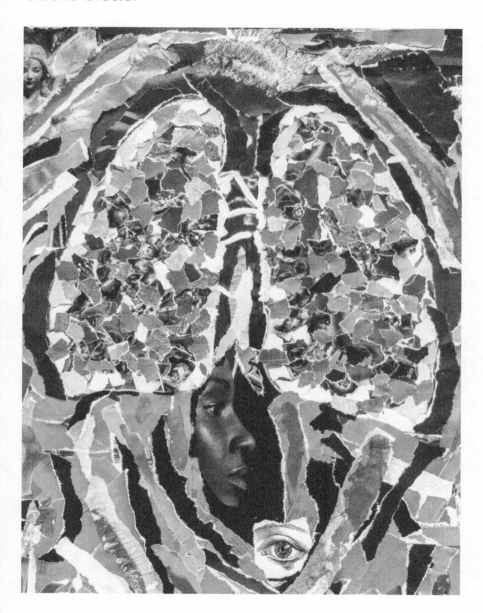

Tumbling

Merril D. Smith

I dream I'm Alice tumbling

down
down
down
the rabbit hole.

The White Rabbit says he's late,
but I've lost track of the days,

stuck in a recurring nightmare,

this upside-down world of Mad Hatters and despots,
where the large things become small and the small things
    large,
the tiny fires of hate grow into
pogroms, cross burnings, and small signs reading
 "no colored, no Jews, no dogs"
turn into strange fruit.

People gather, protest, seek a place at the table.
But the teapot is empty
the dormouse sleeps, stunned by gas(lighting)

a blaze, a flash--

As the World Burns

the Queen of Hearts shouts "off with their heads,"
she holds a bible.
It's all optics, you know? The courtiers nod

and more bodies fall
down
down
down

It's the moment when I should wake,
but I think I'm still caught in this dream,
upside-down
looking up at the sun
seeking a way out.

Trying to breathe.

Pigmentation / Inclusive Separation
Marvlyn C. Vincent

Black, white,
dark, light.
First thing noticed about another.
For some, no knowledge is needed,
they do not need to look no further.
we're defined by pigment,
judged by color.
On a form we're asked to pick one or another,
and if you're mixed,
yeah, your category still exists,
that one's called other.
There is no longer required segregation,
but based on this system
there is a design.
A clearly defined line.
A reminder of another time,
one firmly embedded in our heart and mind.
They say we're all included,
no longer segregated, divided or excluded.
That over the years we've made our case,
proved, that we're all part
of the human race.
That our lives are all of equal value,
no matter the shade, the color, the hue.
I speak for myself,
I don't know about you.
But to them my color, still determines my value.

Thin Blue Lie
F.I. Goldhaber

Not peace officers.
Bullies in uniform.
Demand that protesters stop
impeding vehicle traffic,
then block the same streets just vacated.
Close the sidewalks so demonstrators have
nowhere to go. Always making excuses
to attack with weapons of war: tanks, grenades, smoke
bombs, batons, sonic cannons, chemicals, poison gas.
No regard for law, civil rights, any consequences.
Injuring and arresting journalists, lawyers, civilians.
Blatantly lying the next morning, claiming dissidents engaged
in criminal acts of violence, throwing projectiles at police.
When in truth, the only assaults, shootings, riots, and other
    carnage were
committed by police who put lives, safety, and the First
    Amendment at risk.

Hush
John Cochrane

Chorus:

Hush, little baby, don't you cry,
No matter who wins, we're all gonna die.

I remember almost four years ago,
Kate McKinnon playing piano
and singing "Hallelujah" on SNL,
acknowledging The Loss, with grace.
I remember crying that night,
But I wasn't in fear for my life.
Not yet.
I'm white, like Kate. We always manage.

CHORUS

In January 2017 I was pushing my cart of groceries to my car,
when I saw two men ripping my Hillary Clinton bumper sticker off
    my bumper.
I told them to stop,
And they stood up in a very nonchalant, unhurried way, and said,
"Ain't you heard, bitch? This cunt lost. You don't wanna be lettin'
    folks know you voted for her,
do ya? 'Cause some folks, they might take it the *wrong way*."
By now his face was just inches from mine as he was leaning in.
Towering over me,
Glowering,
hatred and beer on his breath,
Chewing tobacco spittle flowing out of one side of his mouth,
A rancid odor wafting from every pore of his body,

As the World Burns

And that damned, damned red cap topping it off.
That rattled me.
I told my husband about it that night and he told me not to worry
about two drunken rednecks.

CHORUS

We talked it over and over and over.
We talked it to death.
I was against the idea, and he was for it.
But part of me wanted it, too, and I was 34 years old already.
So in 2018 we crossed our fingers and started our family.
And in April of 2019 we welcomed our beautiful biracial baby boy
into the world.
Happy day of birth, Joseph!
We sang him lullabies, and I, at least, was able to forget,
For awhile,
The scenes which were getting progressively worse every day.

CHORUS

When COVID hit earlier this year,
I had already quit my job to be a stay-at-home Mom,
A decision we'd made jointly, and gone over our financial
numbers thoroughly.
Then my husband's construction business shut down, too many
guys ignoring all the warnings,
All the guidelines,
Still going out after work drinking,
Having backyard cookouts with the neighbors,
All that bullshit.
My husband wore masks and gloves
As long as he had that job…
But that wasn't very long into it.

War

We got the ONE stimulus check.
No unemployment, no unemployment augmentation.
There's a backlog of applications,
And because our state's one of the hardest hit,
No telling when they might get processed.
I've never seen my husband so upset.
Pacing our home like a wild animal in a cage.
So when the protests started,
He was there every afternoon and night,
Even though I begged him to not go.
I told him that I needed him, our son needed him.
All he could say was,
"Babe, this is bigger than just our family, this is OUR TIME. I have
    to go.
I have to make a difference."
I would wait until I put little Joseph to sleep,
Then I would worry about him,
And usually cry,
And sometimes get some sleep,
And some nights not.
Until he made it home the next day.

CHORUS

Until he didn't make it home the next day.
A patrol car came by our home.
Two very polite officers,
One white, one black,
Said there had been an accident involving my husband,
And would I come with them, please.
I called my mother to come watch Joseph,
And she was there within ten minutes.
She lives a twenty-minute drive away.

As the World Burns

Then, somehow, we were in the patrol car,
And though I've never been to the police station before,
I knew we'd just passed it.
I told them, wait, we just passed the station,
And they said "Yes ma'am, we just need to make one stop first."
And I knew.
And I vomited violently in the back seat.
And I very distinctly remember
(I will remember this until my dying day)
The white cop said, "Oh Jesus Christ, she's a puker. I ain't
   cleaning that shit up."

CHORUS

They had to drag me out of the car when we got to the morgue
And yes it was him
Of course it was him
And his teeth were knocked out
Those beautiful, white, evenly-spaced,
Never-smoked-a-cigarette-in-his-life teeth
Were missing and broken off
And his lips were cut and bruised
And one eye socket was eyeless and about the size of a fist
With tiny bits of bone fragments still glittering
Around the open gray wound that I was later told was his brain
And as horrible as it all was
I threw myself on his body
Wanting to touch him one last time
And so of course they dragged me off him and back into the car,
   handcuffed this time
"for my own protection" to slide around in my own vomit.

War

CHORUS

When we got to the station
The two cops turned me over to a female cop,
Who glared daggers at them, uncuffed me,
Took me to a restroom and helped me clean up.
I was taken to an office where a black Sergeant sat behind a
    desk,
With a white officer sitting in a chair next to mine,
where I did not immediately see his face.
The sergeant explained how the demonstrators had charged the
    police lines,
And police had responded with batons and rifle butts,
Non-lethal force, you understand,
But that one or two officers had fired their rubber bullet guns,
Not using proper procedures,
Which is to force the projectile to bounce before it hit a target,
But in a very few cases,
Right at a protestor's face.
The white officer turned to face me and said,
"I didn't mean nothin' of it. I shore am sorry, Mrs."
And this time, his breath didn't stink of beer,
And he'd showered,
But it was him.

CHORUS

Rant
Irma Do

I could rant about the boredom
About not being able to eat at the crepe place
Or get my nails done to match the front door
I could rant about the kids
Running around inside then outside, being loud
And disturbing the neighbors working from home
I could rant about the heat
And not being able to go to the beach
Or to Disney for the first time
I could rant, but I won't
I can't
When families are made newly homeless through job loss
When food pantries are not getting enough donations as their
    lines get longer
When parents are risking their lives for $7.25 an hour
When some kids don't have an outside
When some kids can't be loud or else
When black bodies are pitted against blue bodies
When black bodies are killed and will never get to go to Disney

My immigrant, light skinned Asian, college educated, middle
class, suburban stay at home mother runner rant is bullshit.

Because I can still breathe when others cannot.

Blackout Art II

D. M. Burton

"And I like it."

"When we were discussing this yesterday, we talked about him as if he were some sort of hired killer."

"It sounds far-fetched, I know, but—"

"It struck me that there is so little background on him it seems almost like a smokescreen. Both IB and SIS established cover companies outside the building in the fifties and sixties."

"I was wondering when you'd think of that," Edklinth said.

"I'd has ermissidy too through the personnel files from much," Figuerola said.

"No," Edklinth said, shaking his head. "We can't go into the archives without authorization from the has pet of Secretariat, and we don't want to attract attention until we have more to go on."

"So what next?"

"Mårtensson," Edklinth said. "Find much, he's working on."

Salander was studying the vent window in her room when they d the key turn in the door. In came Jonasson. It was past on Tuesday night. He had interrupted her kill going how to break before grenska hospital.

She had measured window and discovered that her head would fit through they id that she would not have much problem squeezing the rest of her body through. It try. He storey to he ground, but a combination of torn sheets and a ten-foot extension cord from a floor lamp would solve that problem.

She had plotted her escape step by step. The problem was what she would wear. She had underwear, a hospital nightshirt, and a pair of plastic flip-flops that she had managed to borrow. She had 200 kronor in cash from Annika Gi They pay for from the hospital snack shop. That should be enough cheap p are jeans and a T-shirt at the Salvation Army store, if she could find one in Göteborg. She would have to spend what was left of the money on a call to Plague, a fellow member of Hacker Republic. Than everything would work out. She planned on landing in Gibril be are ays after she escaped, and from here she would create a new where in the world.

Jonasson sat in the guest chair. She sat on the edge of her bed.

"Hello, Lisbeth. I'm sorry I haven't come to see you the past five days, but I've been up to my ears in the ER, and I've also been made a mentor for a couple of interns."

Tuesday, May 17

Figuerola woke at 6:10 on Tuesday morning, took a long run along Norr Mälarstrand, showered, and clocked in at police headquarters at 8:10. She prepared a memorandum on the conclusions she had reached the day before.

At 9:00 Edklinth arrived, giving him twenty minutes to deal with his mail, then knocked on his door. She waited while he read her four pages. At last he looked up.

"The chief of Secretariat," he said.

"He must have approved loaning out Mårtensson. So he must know that Mårtensson is not at Counter-Espionage, even though according to Personal Protection that's where he is."

Edklinth took off his glasses and polished them thoroughly with a paper napkin. He had met Chief of Secretariat Shenke at meeting and internal conferences on countless occasions, but he couldn't claim to know the man well. Shenke was rather short, with thin reddish-blond hair and a waistline that had expanded over the years. He was no doubt fifty-five and had worked at SIS for at least twenty-five years, possibly longer. He had been chief of Secretariat for a decade, and was assistant chief before that. Edklinth thought of him as a taciturn man who could act ruthlessly when necessary. He had no idea what he did in his free time, but he had a memory of having once seen him in the garage of the police building in casual clothes, with a golf bag slung over his shoulder. He had also run into him once at the opera.

"There's one thing that struck me," Figuerola said.

"What's that?"

"Evert Gullberg. He did his military service in the forties and became a tax attorney, and then in the fifties he vanished into thin air."

A Nation in Chokehold
Megha Sood

The streets are overcrowded
lanes are bustling with protest
thrumming with anger
overcrowded bus stops, sidewalks, bike lanes, parks
brimming and spilling with pain
Unfettered;
Uncontrolled

Everywhere now should be quarantine
where the lanes should be deserted
where everyone should be   *six feet apart*
masks covered mouths but still breathing
with breaths laced with privilege

Here the nation recalls the pain
the unanswered angst of those calling from the grave
for those grieving souls who are yet to put at rest
those headstones, now a place maker for a black mother
to sit and cry alone in the deep folds of the night

Here the nation mirrors the screams
of the black blood lacing the sidewalks
mouth gaping at the nakedness of the whole nation
staring back at the end of a gun   *a police gun*

Here the nation acknowledges the police shooting went awry
here the nation recalls how the protectors devour
here the nation recalls how easy it is for you to forget

As the World Burns

a loss of life and wait for the next news cycle to begin
Here the nation recalls how eyes pop out
losing life in an instant:
when your brain misses the next wave
of life-giving air coursing through your veins

Here the nation recalls how the brutal hands
loaded with power thick as greed,
dripping with incessant hunger
took lives boisterously

Here the nation recalls how life was ignored
leaving the warm and supple body
on the sidewalks pitted with fear and blood
of the beautiful black bodies

Here the nation recalls how to survive
by sucking in, gulping air
taking deep long breaths feverishly
trying to survive after being
in a chokehold for 8.5 minutes

Here the nation remembers Eric Garner
Here the nation learns again how to   *breathe*
freely

Waterloo (George Floyd)
Johann Morton, Morton Labs

Breathe
Matthew D. Eayre

It's a long walk to the car
And I see red and blue
lights ahead
Maybe you should walk on
the other side of the street
Because my mouth is full
of bullets
And this storm is going
straight out of the
atmosphere, babe
I'll regrow my teeth after I
grind them to pieces, my
tongue won't get in the way
They won't see my teeth in
my hand
But they want to, they're
laughing
The cute girls in their
cruelty
And the blue men are
waiting
For my blood
I've got a muscle spasm
somewhere near my fourth
rib and I can't breathe
carefully anymore
Before I wake
I've got teeth to chew

War

And I can't stop until I let
these words breathe

Ebony
Hanlie Robbertse

You carved the color of my skin into a sin so that the world
    could see:
slave, robber, crook, murderer, unclean, unworthy… some
of the words you shaped around my dermis. Justified you've
stood in your superior view-deserving in your prosperity and
I stampeded into a hazy comfort of perceived righteousness
and valor when you abolished your prejudice and tried to
silence your conscience of guilt. Yet, I remained on the fringe
of the spectrum and the right to live humanely has been in
your hands-how swiftly you endeavor to mete out judgement.
You owned the right to kill me for no reason other than your
inherited stereotype of what you made me until one day
I lay under your oppressive knee pleading for air while dying.
And as my final gasp of air resonated over the earth, finally
others were shaken from their fog of compliance and
    ignorance,
and as a wave humanity said, "These lives matter and we can't
be silent anymore." From my last breath was borne a new
    revolution
that will hopefully shake loose the shackles of labels that have
    been slapped
onto many that said "Wrong color" and thus subjugated them
    into a life
of living in fear. And one day, when others remember me, may
    it be
as a moment when the world stood up and said: "We will no
    more judge according to color,
but by the deeds that you've enacted in your life."

Tightrope
Elle Arra

Suspended above the day's mundanity and slog,
an ever-present tightrope
black bodies traverse in tandem.
It's like navigating an ocean built
almost entirely of undertow
while maintaining stride and heft of dreams.

We are not permitted our hysteria
not without it being labeled non sequitur rage.

As the World Burns

We walk this tightrope
lilting between full bloom
and languish,
walk with bullets in our backs,
twine around our necks,
asphalt under our skin,
knees on our windpipes,
tree branches in our hair,
blood like rubies cascading,
splayed bone like smooth porcelain,
black skin – ribbons and ribbons,
afro confetti—

War

Sunday, August 16, 2020. I walked the four corners of US 72 and Wall Triana [in Madison County, Alabama] where giant signs were hoisted in peaceful protest of the shooting of Dana Fletcher 10 months earlier. I took photos and spoke with his wife and mother who have had to wedge their grief and mourning between breathing and fighting for justice. I cannot imagine having to take moments meant for private sorrows to fight publicly for transparency—the human and decent thing being denied them.

I watched Dana's now fatherless daughter playing in the grass while her mother, grandmother, and a sizable group gave everything they had to this effort. I took it all in–the focus on their faces, the bullhorn call and response, and the raised signs calling for justice.

It was extremely hot and humid that late morning/early afternoon, but the dedicated group spent three hours occupying the four corners of the intersection adjacent to the lot where Dana was killed. People from all walks of life honked as they drove by and elevated their fists through car windows in solidarity. Several vehicles pulled up and gifted cold, refreshing, electrolyte drinks to the protestors. There was beauty in the coming together despite the bitter reasons for the gathering; there was beauty in the union of people of all colors and lifestyles for one common goal.

On October 27, 2019 Dana Fletcher was fatally shot by a Madison police officer in front of his wife and daughter. Nearly a year later, there still has been no transparency in this matter. According to Alabama law, body camera footage is privileged information, so the District Attorney refuses to release the footage or the alleged 911 call that precipitated Fletcher's death. Stills from the incident have been released, but these stills do not reveal the whole story.

You can help. Please go to change.org and sign the petition to enact the Dana Fletcher bill making bodycam footage public record.

https://www.change.org/p/alabama-state-house-enact-the-dana-fletcher-bill-making-body-cam-video-footage-public-record

War

We walk that tightrope,
   what a beautiful gait.
—even our dying is a glorious walk home.

Kneeling in the Bean Vault at Sunset
Hokis

What would happen if America fell quiet?

No more wasted energy
biting heads off mind-less Cheetos
nor offering skulls to crack with canisters.

What if then a secret underground resurrected?

Paintings of boldly colored coded quilts brushed buildings.
Assimilated folklore with covert directives for uploading images
of mailed-in ballots to a private Instagram page.

Today's freedom riders would fill the backup thumb drive
transport and store it in the Svalbard global seed vault
with all the other drastic measures
that our righteously beloved must continue to dream of.

That chip of truth would kneel
beside all species of beans
while we eat crow in silence,
waiting for the moment in the day we know will come.

Mourning.

Flora

Tamara J. Madison

For them noosed and strung
from your withering family tree,
catching searing razor or metallic seed
between jewels, teeth or spleen,
crosses aflame upon the scars of their backs—
with one blink of the sun,
stars shed their skins
instead of tears.
The sloughs slip
among the heavenly bodies,
drift on crippled winds, wriggle
through the whimpering willows' leaves,
land softly on a regiment
of weeds bending
to bear them as honors
before they slip again
to hardened soil yet fecund
with prophecy.

Titanium threads root,
silver stems ascend,
concrete contracts, splits
as copper waters birth
crowning heads
of cast iron roses.

Rhetoric(al)
Hokis

Have we
hung ourselves
on our age
old tree of history
In the deep south
the red south,
the bloody red
on the deep state
Patched with liquid gold
by hammer and
the remains of enslaved
sickle cells?

What Happened?

A Golden Shovel Poem after Langston Hughes
Melissa Fadul

Tell me son, what
the hell happened
in the South to
you after you escaped a-
gain. No, Mama— tell me your dream
what you've deferred?
Deferred? What does—
Postpone is what it
means, mama. So mama, what's been dry
in you all this time? What needs to wake up?
What were your master's lashes like?
How did you not fall a-
part? Mama, did you ever find a raisin
amongst grapes in the field— hide it in
your pocket? Kneel in corn stalks to escape the heat?
Did you make dolls from corn shucks in the sun?

Son, I kneeled on cotton in the fields or
dreamed of bathin' in the river. But you know, hope fester.
Mostly, I thought of you—what it would be like
not to wonder where you is, not to feel like you was a
limb on me that I couldn't touch because it was sore.
I wrote you letters. I sliced my skin and
dropped my blood into a pot and then
dipped my fingers in and run
them across the page. Does
that seem like enough for you? It

As the World Burns

hurt. And you know, blood stink.
Poundings from whippings turned gangrene, stunk like
pus and vomit, rotten.
I was just meat.
I thought my masta' would chop me up or
hell, I was gonna do it myself. Let my body crust,
and air dry in this heat invented by the white man and
it'd lay like a dead cricket . Its sugar
song, gone foreva'— over.
Hours moved slow like
daylight stuck at dusk—a
night's doily dying to drape over a syrupy
land—it never turned dark. I prayed for sweet
evening to cover scars—I'd say to myself, maybe
it come. It didn't. Twilight was a scab. It,
a curtain that just—
imagine a sky that sags
waiting for a spine. Once, I saw a woman's back beaten like
it was dough. He sliced her with a
knife and she bled out heavy
clots. That night I tried to steal and load
my masta's gun. I just wanted to hol' it or
prove I could. That wrong? Does
that sound bad? Does it?

Everyone needs to explode.

Dodger, Black and White Snapshot, *Ebbets Field, Brooklyn*, 1955

Melissa Fadul

Robinson sneaks down third
    steel cleats spike and pound the powdered foul line
Jackie jets for home in cotton pants and dives
    around the masked catcher
as his hand slides across the base
    The umpire spots Jackie's print on home plate,
spreads his arms and yells,
    SAFE!

As the World Burns

July 2020
Sally Zakariya

What you can see reflected
in the broken store window:
the policeman's shield and club
the black man in handcuffs
the protester's sign

What you can hear on a city street:
the explosion of the flash-bang
the ricochet of the rubber bullet
the cries of *I can't breathe*

What you can feel this night:
the upwelling of sorrow and anger
the resolve to change things at last
to somehow make America the nation
it always should have been

    The last time I saw soldiers
    in D.C. way back in '68
    you said they hassled you
    when you walked up 18th Street
    to see me but when we were together
    black guy and white girl
    they frowned but let us pass

What I know fifty-some years later:
time to change things at long last

Jackrabbits
Katherine DeGilio

There is a wooden bar at the end of the block,
with a sign naming the place Jackrabbits,
though I've never seen any such creature in the vicinity,

Behind the parched oak of the store, and the tired stone of the other,
an alleyway forms into an abyss, where purgatory lingers
between smoky laughter and the ring of a corner store.

Across the way, on my childhood bicycle,
I avoid the alleyway like a crack on the sidewalk.
My converse push down each pedal, and a head smacks
against the bricks.

I close my eyes but do not need them to know
how slurs ruminate against the two buildings like a thick soup,
stirred by an unassuming grandmother who just doesn't know better.

Past the line between right and wrong, and down the lane,
the alleyway is a place for liminal morality,
where the sound of a fist, harmonizes with childhood laughter.

As my adolescence groans against the spaciousness of spring,
I can hear a couple arguing between the stores.
The woman's voice starts to crack until it doesn't exist.

As the World Burns

Through the colors of autumn, red and blue lights flash past the
alleyway.
It is not a place for stopping. There is no assault.
There is only teaching them a lesson, which only God sees.

I ride to the end of the town, the line I fantasize about crossing.
Under the name is a single sentence: A Town with Love,
though I've never seen any such thing in the vicinity.

Divide and conquer

Carla Toney

The changing face of dispossesssion

While everyone has heard of Chernobyl, Fukushima, and the three-quarters reactor core meltdown at Three Mile Island, who has heard of the Church Rock uranium mill tailings spill that happened in the same year, on 16 July 1979 when "1100 thousand tons of radioactive sludge in 94 million gallons of radioactive waste water including highly radioactive decay products of uranium . . . flowed off the private United Nuclear site onto the Navajo Reservation." There was no national outcry as it affected "[r]ural, Native, Latino, and low-income Anglos." Their water was poisoned and they are still living with the "devastation of cancer, and the footprints of other non-cancer radiation impacts from the 1979 event."

In 2016, the Standing Rock Sioux Tribe of North Dakota drew the world's attention when they initiated protests to protect their land and water resources from the Dakota Access pipeline. And in August 2020, during the worldwide coronavirus pandemic, federal and state authorities claimed that the Great Sioux Nation does not have the right to set up checkpoints to determine who they will allow to pass onto and through their tribal lands.

In the 21st century, dispossession no longer means federal soldiers rounding up thousands of First Nations peoples and forcing them to march a thousand miles while the sick, the weak, and the old die by the side of the road. But it does mean the "act of depriving someone of land, property, or other possessions," of refusing to grant Native Americans rights over their own property, of failing to protect them and their lands from the abuses of private firms and corporate capitalism, and of neglecting to pay them for the resources that are extracted from their lands.

The changing face of slavery

As soon as African-Americans were no longer owned by and subjected to the whims of white masters, new crime laws, prisons, and the convict lease system were introduced. The promises of forty acres of land and the loan of mules, made to former slaves at the conclusion of the Civil War as restitution for their labor in building the nation, were withdrawn; the land was given to their former masters; and former slaves were faced with another set of appalling conditions. "Southern criminal laws increased sharply the penalty for petty theft" (Foner 1988, 70-71, 593).

> "[T]he sole concern of law enforcement seemed to be to protect property owned by whites. South Carolina made arson a capital offense, mandated life imprisonment for burglary, and increased drastically the penalty for the theft of livestock. In North Carolina and Virginia, charged one black spokesman, 'they send [a man] to the penitentiary if he steals a chicken.' Mississippi's famous 'pig law' [of 1876] defined the theft of any cattle or swine as grand larceny punishable by five years in jail. 'It looks to me,' commented a black resident of the state, 'that the white people are putting in prison all that they can get their hand on" (Foner 1988, 594).

From petty crimes and misdemeanors to the war on drugs, there has been an overinvestment in criminalization and the militarization of the police in the United States. Referring to the prison-industrial complex, Angela Davis states: "In California, whose prison system is the largest in the country and one of the largest in the world, the passage of an inmate labor initiative in 1990 has presented businesses seeking cheap labor with opportunities uncannily similar to those in Third World countries" (Lubiano, 1997, 272-273).

Hanging for a hog, a shilling (12 pence) for rape

White rulers "willfully helped create … antagonism between Indians and Negroes in order to preserve themselves and their privileges." To ensure that poor whites, blacks and Indians would never come together and to prevent all contact and communication between white servants, Native Americans and blacks, on the 15th of August 1701 the South Carolina Commons House of Assembly advised that "no Servant [white] or Slave [black] be sent beyond the Savanna Town."

This backcountry was a violent region where murders and assaults were more than five times as common as crimes against property. The Hatfield-McCoy feud (1863-1891) "over two razorback hogs …led to the killing of twenty people and the wounding of at least twenty more." In Cumberland County, Virginia, the punishment for hog stealing was death by hanging. For the rape of an eleven year old girl the punishment was a fine of one shilling (Fischer 1989, 768).

Today's tragedy

The rich, bellies bloated, devoured the New World's land, resources, wealth. Africans were enslaved. Indians were dispossessed. The poor, black slaves, white indentured servants scrabbled for crumbs from their table. Struggling to feed themselves, their loved ones, these peoples all too often fought each other.

Today's tragedy? Nothing has changed. The wealthy are a thousand, a million times richer than ever, and the poor are still scrabbling, and fighting each other against their own best interests.

With extracts from *No Man's Land: "Multitribal Indians" in the United States* by Carla Toney (2019).

---

[1] Mary Olson. "Church Rock, NM: Living with North America's Worst Nuclear Disaster for 39 Years." *Nuclear Information and Resource Service.* Accessed 18 June 2020: https://www.nirs.org/church-rock-nm-living-with-north-americas-worst-nuclear-disaster-for-39-years/

[2] Mike Faith. "Our fight against the Dakota Access pipeline is far from over." *Guardian.* 15 November 2019. https://www.theguardian.com/commentisfree/2019/nov/15/dakota-access-pipeline-standing-rock

Nina Lakhani. "Dakota access pipeline: court strikes down permits in victory for Standing Rock Sioux." *Guardian.* 26 March 2020. https://www.theguardian.com/us-news/2020/mar/25/dakota-access-pipeline-permits-court-standing-rock

[3] William S. Willis, "Divide and Rule: Red, White and Black in the Southeast," *The Journal of Negro History,* XLVIII, 1963, p. 158.

[4] See James H. Easterby. *South Carolina Commons House of Assembly Journal.* August 15, 1701, p. 8. Savannah Town was six miles below the site of present-day Augusta, Georgia on the Carolina side of the Savannah River.

A Quick Rant on the Notion of Supremacy
Philip Vernon, MA

The most pressing discussion in the Western world is how right-wing nationalism can represent the "*supremacy*" of a global minority group (Europe and those spawned therefrom) who only represent roughly 18% of the planet and who spent the better part of the 16th-century to present robbing, looting, pillaging, and eradicating the socio-economic structures of societies around the globe. Along with neofeudal-induced climate change (unsustainable capitalism), perhaps such Western created social disorder borne of both colonialism and post-colonialism also more than anything else speaks to global migration crises! If the other 82% of the planet ever seek post-colonial "payback" (be it simply a denial of coveted resources or a more direct manifestation thereof) we, those of European descent, are in for a world of hurt . . .

. . . Or if one wants to take a Biblical take on the same concept; it is the *meek who shall inherit the earth*. By any definition, we of European descent are not likely to be seen as "meek" and we are therefore equally screwed!

. . . And it is most paradoxical that the United States, who due to its "founding" as an immigrant country and soon its status as a *majority* "minority" nation (resembling the global collective within a state), should be best positioned to act as both buffer and more importantly a bridge away from a hostile form of global "payback".

. . . But herein, we too are foregoing our potential contribution toward lasting **"exceptionalism"** — a type of ***human supremacy*** — as we are being sucked into the vortex of delusions of an antiquated global minority and ideologies which undergird its fragile existence.

Weaving
Tamara J. Madison

She loathes them.

Americans. Wishes she could find one.
Shred it to pieces to weave her mourning veil.

A horrid Black Hawk,
ripping her meager piece
of alkebulanian sky, hovered
to lay its poisonous eggs.

The village could not find enough
of her three-year old
to bury.

Her eyes twitch.
Her fingers twiddle.
The starving loom waits.

If We Burn
Robert Okaji

What flares instead to replace our
privileged nights? And which

assemblage of words could reorder these
deaths into comprehension,

change *I can't breathe* from epitaph
to actuated plea for help?

Are words ever enough?
Can we stack our indifference and fear

into a mile-high pyre, and torching it
watch them rise to nothingness,

disappearing through the clouds
into the streaming light of cold, dark stars?

Raise your hands and sing. Blow softly
upon the ember. Inhale and recall.

Do you still feel? Will you breathe?
Every fire needs oxygen.

"If We Burn" was originally published in *If Your Matter Could Reform*,
chapbook, Dink Press, 2015.

"Your Guilt is Not Your Ticket Out of This Room"

After watching If These Halls Could Talk by Lee Mun Wah

Tia M. Hudson

Circle of people, circle of eyes
Asian- to African- to Latina-
to Muslim- to white-
American.
Finally, finally, somewhere
the conversation starts
until a bit of truth
a tiny sliver
when one white man says
"I never saw you as fully human"
in tears, unbelieving, but
driven to truth
and dies a bit
because finally, finally
he realizes how others have died
to themselves
to accommodate him.

One woman faces him
She does not forgive;
she does not erase
his shame.
She tells him the truth–
a sliver of the truth;
no forgiveness here,
just the reality of his chains
trying, trying, falling, getting up

As the World Burns

trying again
until he does not know
why he gets up again.
She tells him the bitter truth
"We are in a war for our humanity."

On Breonna Taylor's Birthday

June 5, 2020
Teresa T. Chappell

I keep giving myself stress fevers,
registering at a low 99.4 degrees --
not high enough to warrant care. Yet,
I feel chills, and wear sweatsuits in the muggy
80 degree heat. I wrap myself in a down blanket
and sleep. And I feel guilty
for sleeping because sleeping
is not going to help Breonna Taylor
get justice. She was asleep and
never woke up. I have to
wake up. Stop sleepwalking.
There is a war that needs
to be won. Girl, -- I'm talking
to myself. Is that a symptom
of a fever? Or rage?—they need you
on the front lines. Cops have a harder time
beating white women in public.
Girl, this is your fever speaking,
made up of unrest and white guilt.

"Nice" People
F.I. Goldhaber

Germans who collaborated,
who turned away from the horror,
may have been thought ordinary
citizens. But they were not "nice".

There are no "well-meaning" racists,
"kind" white supremacists, "sweetheart"
homomisiasts, or "good guy"
misogynists. They are not "nice".

Those who choose to look the other
way, to ignore politics, and
to focus on happier things
are not "nice". They are complicit.

They may want to believe they are
"nice". If you are related, you
may want to believe they are "nice".
But, oppression is never "nice".

They may be ignorant, they may
claim lack of privilege because
they are poor, uneducated,
disabled. But, they are not "nice".

War

The time has come to choose. Fascist
or Antifa. Capitalist
or socialist. Colonizer
or resistance. In every
case, only the latter is "nice".

ask yourself why?
Linda M. Crate

black lives matter
isn't saying
yours doesn't,
it isn't saying their lives
mean more than yours;
it is a movement meant to bring
justice to those who have
been oppressed
hundreds of years—
i am tired
of people purposefully
misunderstanding,
tired of people insisting that
somehow equality
will give them less a share
of pie;
i am tired of people screaming
that 'all lives matter' or
'blue lives matter'—
cops choose their profession,
a black person doesn't choose the
color of their skin;
and i am so tired of people
twisting things into what they are not—
if it bothers you that black lives matter,
ask yourself why?
if you enjoy black culture, have black friends and family,
and are invested in an inclusive society;
black lives should matter to you.

Contained in My Thoughts
Kimberly Cunningham

I counted stars
I held my breath
Looked away
Searched everywhere
I got a grip
I let things slip

Circumstance came for me
I followed faithfully
Wandered aimlessly
Listened to the gritty,
tinny hum every night

Destination is suspended in pandemonium

I watched selfishly,
dare I say,
dire in questionable conscious
Can the end commence amongst chaos?

Travesty and amnesty collide
or rather coexist
Stuck we are in a glass jar
Hope is the lid

Pass the peas
I need to feel full

Speak the Truth
Sonia Beauchamp

for the space / between black & blue
will never create / a perfect circle
& this lie / through which / we see
our world will soon / awaken
to the red & the blue / lights flashing
tender bruises / against the stain / of flesh
on the butcher's block / searing
pavement / the high noon scars / our soul
across gritty asphalt / open wounds
on the television screen / my children
look into my eyes / & I turn my head
regret the time / spent paralyzed in fear

the lesson they didn't want us to learn
ashley jane

we were taught
to avoid that something in the dark
to run from the ghosts that chase us,
to bathe in all the colors of summer
because the light will heal us
far more than the shadows ever will

they didn't teach us
that it's okay to hide
when everything becomes too much,
when our winter hearts need a break
from a world that camouflages its pain
behind spring-filled eyes and sunshine smiles

we were taught
that we were free to love and live,
that we could be anything we wanted,
that opportunity would present itself
and all we had to do was seize it

they didn't teach us
that love is love is love
only stands true when it meets society's guidelines,
that our choices are our own
but only if they meet the standards
that someone else set for us

As the World Burns

they didn't teach us
that the ground beneath our feet will shake with hate
when we defy the rules we never agreed to follow,
that freedom comes with a price
we might not be willing to pay

no, they didn't teach us that

Revolution
Erin Van Vuren

This world is filled with more
sad stories than water; more
anger than blades of grass.
But what they won't tell you
is there is more magic than
grains of sand; more hope
than mornings began.
What they won't tell you is
you were never meant to be
a tragedy. You are, and always
have been...

a revolution.

- Erin Van Vuren
@papercrumbs

town of betrayal
Aviva Lilith

i was walking on an autumn day,
the leaves not yet ready to
fall to their graves.
i remember seeing boys
they walked in front of me.
one made a sound as if he'd seen
something so grotesque that
it made his stomach
scared of daylight.
soon i passed what the
object was,
it was on the ground
just as the leaves tend to be,
motionless and dead.
a small bird,
beak filled with one last song,
perhaps the boys couldn't hear
what it had to say,
but i listened closely.
i had also seen something
grotesque that day,
but it was not
the little bird with its
foot flat on the pavement
and its wing crumpled,
contorted like a dried leaf;
i saw the grotesque thing
in another form:

War

apathy in humankind.
i picked up a leaf,
a dying leaf,
and placed it over the
little bird, and said to it,
"you sing beautifully".

Apocalypse
Christine E. Ray

the world burns
wild
chaotic
flames licking
at my heels
melts amber
encasing me
drop by
precious drop
preferred armor
for fragile sanity
beginning to blur
bubble
fail
primal scream
growing deep
in my gut
barely suppressed
I teeter
one presidential tweet
one revisionist headline
one bigoted Facebook post
away from bursting
supernova
simultaneously
struck by irony
of how protected
how privileged
this life of mine
really is
wearing accident-of-birth
white
female

War

middle-class skin
with equal parts
grief
shame
self-hatred
relief
I look out
my suburban window
watching mute
while
the world burns. . .

Death Panel
Ruth Bowley

Every and ever night, a placing of a fitful mind to sleep
awaiting me, the prideful bed of exhausting thoughts. . .
swirling about them. . .
'the death panel' and what has been said.
A good book lay knocking at a bias closet, down an
atrophied hall
Since my plague of disconnected thoughts. . . an acidic
response to the fall.

I have scrubbed my virtue pages clean.
Time may have fragmented,
illusions and reality become obscene.
Dusk to dawn have lived a lifetime in the hours dusk to dawn—
where black and white live. . .
where black and white belongs.

When It Happened
Annette Kalandros

We all thought we were safe,
Tucked away in our little caves—
Until the troops came.
Lessons of history
Abandoned, forgot
In the lies of "Oh, that can't happen here."

The Lady with the shackle
Of broken chain
Around her ankle
Stumbled and fell in the harbor
And drowned.
No one saw.

Few noticed
When the troops tore the sword
From the other woman's hands,
Disarming the danger she was.
Tipped her scales into the streets,
Ripped the blindfold from her eyes
To sear them with the gasses
they'd unleashed.

Few citizens seemed to care
In outcry as those silently
Crying for Justice and Liberty
Took a beating.

As the World Burns

Millions stayed home,
Caved away from it all
And said, "They have to keep order."
"It doesn't affect me, anyway."
"I still watch TV and get to eat.
That's all that matters."

Complacency, Ignorance, and Hatred,
The three old friends,
Toiled and troubled
Over the bubbling pot,
Creating the acid
That would
Sizzle through
Layers of skin and muscles to the bone--
Democracy melting like drenched cake.

And too few cared,
And fewer even dared.

#ACAB
Anthony Glenn

Noise drowns out rhetoric in the next room
Headphones cranked up
Drowning out voices repeating
Lies as revelation
Reinforcing
Until the only truth is the lie

Closed doors and silent
Opinions asked anguish
Traps to pounce

They believe only facts which reinforce their hypocrisy
So no facts at all
Just profitable lies
Slung by earnest white faces
And fear cowering in a bunker
Plotting betrayal

Arguments
Hurt looks when told harsh truths
How their hatred affects the relationships with those around
them

As the World Burns

Dams burst
Killers in blue uniforms
Armed to the teeth
Seething with hatred
Told they have authority
And no repercussions
Demonstrate in real time

Cameras raised
Shouting to be heard
Nothing new
But now seen
Again and again

That old experiment
The worst humans aggregate to the place they can exert the
    most brutality
The best intentions stay silent
And the truest few quit rather than be a part
Rather than be complicit
In this river of blood
We can no longer unsee

The King
Sarah Ito

Burn It All Down
Tremaine L. Loadholt

They asked me if I cared
if the world burned down
and I told them the truth,
"I don't give a damn if
it burned all the way down." The
looks I received cut through the
toughest meat and I think to
myself, "They've got something to
chew on now."

The world's been burning
long before 2020; more eyes
are open, more hearts too.
The bruised backs of
my ancestors are the
compasses of hard times--the
maps
to justice. How many of
these righteous-lipped
bigots can say the same?

We are a peaceful people
with decades of misuse
& abuse dangling from
our limbs. Burn the
courthouses. Burn the
precincts. Burn the White
House; we need a cleansing.

War

Take your rubber bullets,
tear gas, militia gear,
and claims of preserving
community to a landfill
that's used to housing shit
and leave it there.
Until equally reigns supreme . . .
Until lies have faced their truths . . .
Until wrong is made right . . .
Burn it down.
Burn it all the way down

Processed
Eric Syrdal

my mind is in torment
my mind cannot rest
I cannot gulp down one more breath of acrid air
sinking in this salty, blood-warm, ocean of inhumanity

continually, floored by the deplorable
my feet have yet to find purchase on the bottom
I kick and I flail to keep my head above it
struggle to fight off the weight of despondency
in the face of monolithic injustice

I saw a woman
she did not look like me, we shared no DNA
we shared no name
she was my sister

she was my mother and my daughter
she was my wife
she was in chains, she was defenseless
she was scared, she was crying
she was surrounded by people and she was utterly alone

she was a woman; a child of the same universe
molecules of star dust in her veins
she was the same as I, she and I were the same
they processed her like livestock at the slaughterhouse
in the booking booth at the jailhouse
she screamed, pleaded

War

they ignored, indifferent
she screamed and they hurt her
she cried and they hurt her more
stop resisting—they said—as they pulled her down by her face
onto the counter

in space barely able to contain one
3 grown men leaned their full weight upon her
they bent her handcuffed hands behind her
they wedged their knees between her legs
stop resisting

she screamed, she cried, she howled
she said, no
her voice leaned its full weight against my heart
and it broke inside my chest

she was my sister
I could not go to her side
I could not defend her
I could not protect her
I could not substitute my flesh, for hers, to free her
my flesh is considered benign, my flesh is considered
    compliant
my flesh does not contain the USDA certified amount of
    melanin
to be considered dangerous

As the World Burns

my flesh has never felt the bite of a handcuff, the impact of a
    baton
nor my neck the crush of a knee
nor my back the sting of a taser
jokes have never been exchanged
while my corpse drains the last of its blood into the ground
beneath the smiles of my executioners

historical privilege speaks for my lack of experience with horror
though I am ignorant, I learn
I must use my voice for my sister when hers has been silenced:

enough.

fight for change
ashley jane

you are years of hopes dashed,
missing wishes hidden behind
bright eyes and sour tongues
full of rage way past its expiration date
your words come quickly,
spilling down streets that run blue
(please don't make any sudden moves)
let me shield you from the hate
i have learned the weight you carry
is too great a burden to bear alone
we will wear poetry as a bandage,
letters and lines once mumbled in silence
now shouted at the top of our lungs,
our voices becoming a hand grenade
in the fight for change

Conscience
Eleanór Knight

The pain screams behind tired eyes
You hold it high for me to see
They poured distractions upon your injury, missing a few
    cracks
They did it well but clearly not well enough
There are souls in need of healing and they cannot be ignored
    anymore
A strength sleeping within you, waiting to jump out
Release the hounds into this unjustified mess
A mess created by evil and laced with hatred many moons ago
Now is the time to be loud in each and every little thing we do
Stillness has become an urgent hunger for justice
It's in our hands to listen and learn
As we stand with our brothers and sisters
There's no room for normal anymore
We'll kick and scream and then maybe find relief
They call me too emotional but at least I have a conscience
You can take my love and you can throw it away
But I will use all I have to fight for this cause
Loving, learning and fighting every single day

Blackout Art III
D. M. Burton

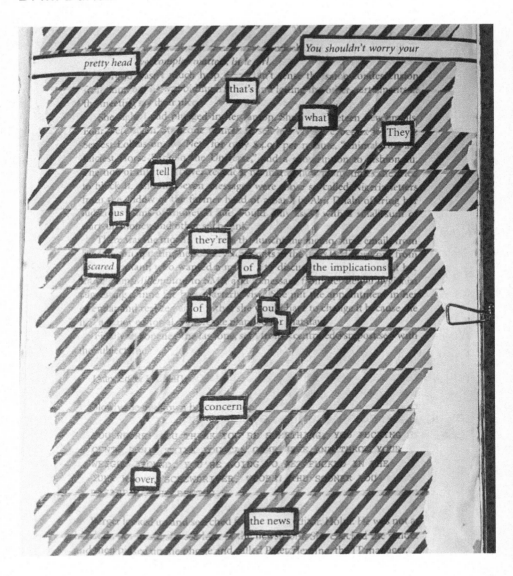

As the World Burns

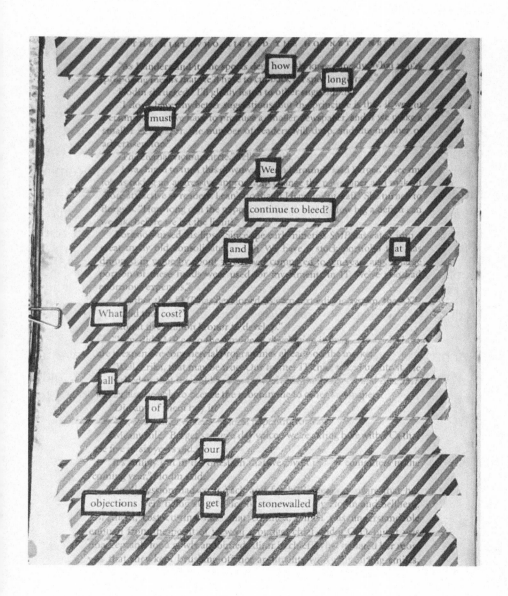

how long must We continue to bleed? and at What did cost? all of our objections get stonewalled

Hauntings
Sarah Doughty

"And the demons I carry with me,
they hide within my eyes."

There's darkness running through these veins. The marrow in my bones echo the screaming coming from my heart. And the demons I carry with me, they walk within my shadow. They hide within my eyes. They speak to me in whispers and remind me of my place. And when my lips quiver and tears sting against my eyes, they roar in triumph. But I am more resilient than them. These broken pieces are jagged and can fight back with the same venom. No matter how beaten down I am, I have more fight within me. I always have more fight left.

Until they're all beaten and silent forever, I'll never stop.

You have the same conviction. Your resilience to never give up is what will be remembered. It will echo through time. If nothing else, remember this: Your voice matters. You matter. Don't let anyone silence your truth.

let the world hear you
ashley jane

you move
through a city dark with despair,
destination unknown
you walk down streets
that have forgotten your name,
parting the shadows with purpose,
a brief visit with the ghosts of those
who passed this way before
but you do not linger,
still fearful of those
who are always watching,
always waiting
the wind carries a message,
both curses and prayers
i listen as you raise your voice,
chanting along with it
i raise my voice, too
perhaps
it will help yours be heard

Status Quo
Susi Bocks

ALL the communities they stomp on have been pounded down
   long enough.
As the oppressed, we've seen and taken abuse in all forms.
Many have died.

We've watched and endured their childish ways.
And been on the receiving end of their vile behavior for way too
   long.
Suffered too much.

The oppressors – all shapes, colors, and forms – have ignored
decency for an eternity.
The torture, the depravity, the madness of their control must
end.
It is **ENOUGH!**

Things must change for the better.
We're done with going two steps forward and six back.
There is no place for them at the table of civility.

ALL who they deem disposable will have their revolution.
They've pushed them too far.
There is a storm coming.

It's time to clear out the rot.
Return the evil to the rocks from under which they crawled out.
May we learn to never repeat the sins of our past.

And may the nefarious never return...

Careful, Love (Your Hate is Showing)
Mandy Kocsis

Careful, love, your hate is showing
Your soul is on the stage
And everyone can see, now
The hatred, and the rage
Careful, love, the curtain's dropped
And the spotlight's brightly trained
On the ugliness you're spreading
All the vitriolic pain
Careful, love, She's watching, too
In all Her magick glory
And you've made yourself a villain
In this sweeping, epic story
Careful, love, Karma's a bitch
And right now She's taking notes
Why, I bet if She were asked, today
She's even got the votes.

Monsters

Marcia J. Weber

the monsters have come out
from their hiding places
dusted the cobwebs off
as they crawled out from under our beds
and the back corners of our closets

those denizens of the dark
have ripped off their white hoods
strut in confidence
down our main streets
and brandish their AKs

how did we get here?
we wail
we thought we had banished them
relegated these barbaric displays
to the shame of our history

so we march and we cry and we pray
as we battle these demons
for the soul our nation
in this fiery summer
of our racial reckoning

The ridding of toxicity during toxic times
Erin Van Vuren

A child will look anyone
in the eye and say,
"This game is no longer fun,"
and simply stop playing it.
Without hesitation.
Without guilt.
And we should still be
doing the same thing.
With bad lovers,
bad friends,
bad jobs...
with the hate we have
for ourselves.
@papercrumbs

- Erin Van Vuren

Persist
Eric Syrdal

We are not yet dragged down upon this field
brave warriors; all
our fate does not lie upon the open ground
as a feast for crows
ours is to struggle
weak-kneed and trembling; aye
but with a strong grip upon the hilt
and a stronger shoulder behind our shields
press on!

Monocultural Haze
Maria Gianna Iannucci

a short leash
pressed arteries
that once choked me
i so could not think
river of submission
i granted permission
when i was blind

and three

children
gather on my diaphragm
to play hide and seek
dizzy and vomiting
on the carousel
of the status quo
i harvest them
from scalding metal frames
cauterizing skinned knees

i speak their real names
in the wake of burning fields
flint and steel
sets us free

A White Woman Asks Herself if She is The One
Ali Grimshaw

who decides your worth
who chooses the distance of your journey
who puts up a fence saying, "you cannot leave"
who imprisons you
who says you are not prepared yet, or ever
who declares the value of your day spent
who gives permission
who dictates the power
who is brave enough for vulnerability
who is willing to see you
who keeps you in a box
who labels you unworthy
who refuses to feel what is truth
who pushes away the body of pain
who wishes to believe that the cycle is over
who forges ahead limping with determined discipline
who doesn't want to go back, and will not
who fights the next step forward after choosing the path
who accepts what doesn't want to be accepted
who will face fear
who will lead
who will trust in following
who will be compassionately bold for all that is and isn't
who will accept responsibility for what you have lived
who will risk believing that it could be different
who will lay down herself as a carpet for the future
who will take a chance and let love in
who will try, try again

For One More Day
Char Trolinder

We live in a world built on the foundation of trauma
Hinged together by hearts and souls
Trying to mortar the cracks with hope and compassion

LA into this state
Marisela Brazfield

reggaeton and Coronavirus-19 blues
seriously woke adverts from podcast sleuths
the AG and the Russia hoax
MSNBC squealin'
through the crumbling ozone
exclusive: thee gospel truth
time doesn't really matter?
eight hundred and seventy-six days gulped Manafort
Prius glide bike lanes wide
out-brake light-mine i'm from LA
bus lights
frozen on Mulholland Drive
Ferrari high beams with movie directors' wives
Tupac karaoking in the car
dope beats Dre interjectin' more more more
memories of seven fo
and the deep state goody two shoes ruse begins
110 N   110 South   360 degrees
the president in forced space
behind JFK's refurbished desk
listening to no one but Fox and Friends
vice president boxing the Fauci and Birx bunch
"Let us love as Jesus has {LOVED?}us."
the archbishop says
yo yo yo!?! does that mean we're all dead…
gentrification gentrification
where's that old voucher to my section-8
extension the PJ's are not communes like Marx's mandate

As the World Burns

meth toad croaks in the trailer park door instead
sweaty poisons seeping into
the young collective American soul
finest tit slash bleach job i ever did see
skyscraper floor path paved with our correctly approved
    recepticled trash
while our slogan puffed chests
at the pride we have at the graves we have filled
behind dumpsters of the riche through their guerilla
drills
as we parade around the good done deeds
the mayor walks those very grounds were 30 years ago
the epidemic shunned back then
but walked for now
took most of my loves forever due to their failure to conform
now today in my home town America-LA country broken down
    to her
DNA
yes Cabal we are openly and freely international with an
admiration for cowboys rudeboys and all the girls in the
world
coexisting vegan meat eater howlers in the night
blues and reds never got us right
media giants you're wrong as fuck about us
we the people of the Westside coast
Chuck wearers Mariachi trumpets duo with Miles
kung fu swinging farmers markets our neighborhoods by far
were never anything 'Little'
Hogs ride wild all the Angels of this Nation
want to say:
America have a very happy birthday
to the sweatshop workers who get paid a dime

War

and to the Chili Peppers the music makers of this bad ass LA
    house
let us not forget the discarded freedom fighters who stand in
    the soup lines
all the kids made from God's rainbow flag of color
and the school babies hanging out at Food 4 Less selling
    candy bars for a dollar
to Kim Soo at my favorite barbecue
and of course Hadib where i used to buy my tokes
and Dona Adelita at the corner with her folks
LaTifah and Darryl who teach me about the Sheppard JC
AJ from the Lakota Nation a Captain America
comic book fiend
and all of my liberal left hook right wing swing coffee house
junkies
let the lights tonight be strong and free
reflecting from Dodger stadium to the ferociously tame
surface of the Silver lake man made designer reservoir

all the little lights
Mela Blust

and all
the little rooftops
how they swallow us
whole

have you ever actually been anywhere?
or is every city, every town
the same hungry mouth, industrial teeth,
corporate heart

smog drowning robin's egg blue
wind carrying poison
mothers raising children who
eat cartoons and watch cereal

scattered broken dolls
give way to backseats and baseball bats
whiskey bottles and regret
both sour on the tongue

how every little soul
stares up
at the same
sky

When This Is Over
Mandy Kocsis

And when this is over
When this has passed
Let's come together
So much better, en masse
Let us remember
The lessons we've learned
This planet we live in
Isn't something we earned
A gift from the cosmos
A place we can live
And for our survival
Do better than this
Lay down your envy
Your self-driven greed
Spread love like a virus
Spread hope like a seed
When this is over
As it one day will be
Just hold one another
And set humanity free
From all of the chains
Anger, hatred, and rage
Leave them behind us
While we turn the next page
I know we can do it
There's no doubt in my mind
We just need to prove it
And now is the time.

Floodlights
John Biscello

We
are the keepers of the sacred fire,
the shapeshifters
and purveyors of starstuff undivided,
We,
tending to flocks of light and clouds,
understand that, come rain or come shine,
the founting marvels
from God's lips, and breadth,
are a flagless scape
containing a ringed inheritance of gospel and blues,
a testimony to grace,
with love our code
and the immutable core nugget
through which we face our shadow
while turned toward the sun,
stepping boldly and bravely
into the glaring unknown.

August
Jane Dougherty

The year has reached the top of the curve
and is on the descent in fits and starts,
unwilling to relinquish the stifling heat. The sun
bows to the inevitable with bad grace,
with a rolling of drums, hurling storm after storm,
crackling lightning through the night,
breaking the darkness into angry fragments.

But it goes, fades, I can feel it in the back
of the air, like the cool light in the eyes,
when the hot tongue promises this is not goodbye.

Biographies

Lisa M. Anderson, PhD is an associate professor of women and gender studies in the School of Social Transformation at Arizona State University. She received her bachelor's from Mount Holyoke College, master's from Smith College, and doctorate in theatre history and criticism from the University of Washington. Her current research interests include the performance of gender; race, gender and sexuality in popular culture; feminist semiotics and phenomenology. Her most recent book, "Black Feminism in Contemporary Drama," was published by University of Illinois Press in 2008. She is currently working on a project with University of Nebraska press on black women, power, and representation in television. She teaches graduate and undergraduate courses on feminist theory, film, representation, and performance in WGS.

Elle Arra, a Michigan native, is a visual artist, poet, and writer currently working and residing in the sultry foothills of the Appalachian Mountains in Madison, AL. Graduating Magna Cum Laude from the HBCU Oakwood University as a "late bloomer – over the age of 40" is something she takes great pride in and has inspired her to create a forthcoming scholarship for other women over the age of 40 endeavoring to complete higher education. Her work has been published in print and online publications such as Hypertrophic Literary, Figroot Press, Corvus Review, The Valley Planet, and more. She also wrote the foreword "Native and Alien" for the book "Some Days, Here" a collection of poems by Tricia De Jesus-Gutierrez. On a given day you can find her tending peonies, freestyling or flowing (mostly 90s golden era hip-hop), watching live theatre, or decorating something– reminding us that style and beauty matter.

Kindra M. Austin is an author and co-founder of Indie Blu(e) Publishing. Austin is an advocate for mental health awareness, sexual trauma survivors, and for the LGBTQ community. She writes from the state of Michigan, where she was born and raised. Her debut novel was released in 2017; she has since written and published two other novels, as well as four poetry collections. Other Indie Blu(e) publications include contributions to We Will Not Be Silenced, and SMITTEN; Austin has also written for The Mansfield Pride magazine, an annual periodical out of Ohio. You can find her books at Amazon, Barnes and Noble online, and at other major online retailers.

Jaya Avendel is a young writer living in the Blue Ridge Mountains of Virginia, where she mingles family and prose. Her work has been published at Visual Verse, Free Verse Revolution, and Spillwords Press, among other publications. She can be found on Twitter as @AvendelJaya.

Sonia Beauchamp (she/her) is a healing artist on the North Shore of Oahu and the daughter of a Chinese immigrant. Read her recent work in Detritus and Re-Side. When she's not writing, she is surrounded by feral chickens in the moonlight. Find out more at www.soniakb.com.

Kim D. Bailey is a published author of poetry, fiction, and nonfiction. Her work has appeared in several online and print journals, podcasts, and anthologies. She has held columnist and editorial positions as well. Kim currently lives and works in Pennsylvania. She shares this journey with her partner Barry, a professional musician and band front man. They write and play songs, nurture their plants and kitties, and get to the beach whenever possible.

Henri Bensussen's poems and stories have appeared in *Eclipse, Blue Mesa Review, Into the Teeth of the Wind,* and others, and in the anthologies, *Beyond the Yellow Wallpaper: New Tales of Madness,* and Lisa Locasio, ed., *Golden State 2017*; a chapbook of poems, *Earning Colors,* was published by Finishing Line Press in 2014. She has a B.A. in Biology from Univ. of California Santa Cruz. Her memoir is looking for a publisher.

Patricia Q. Bidar is a native Californian with family roots in New Mexico, Utah, and Arizona. Her stories have appeared in The Pinch, SmokeLong Quarterly, Little Patuxent Review, Wigleaf, and Pithead Chapel. Apart from fiction, Patricia ghostwrites for progressive nonprofit organizations. She lives with her partner in the San Francisco East Bay.

Sarah Bigham is the author of Kind Chemist Wife: Musings at 3 a.m. She lives in Maryland with her wife, three independent cats, an unwieldy herb garden, several chronic pain conditions, and near-constant outrage at the general state of the world tempered with love for those doing their best to make a difference. Writing, painting, and teaching keep her occupied. Find her at www.sgbigham.com.

Originally from Brooklyn, NY, novelist, poet, performer, and playwright, **John Biscello**, has called Taos, New Mexico home since 2001. He is the author of three novels: Broken Land, Raking the Dust, and Nocturne Variations; a collection of stories, Freeze Tag; two poetry collections Arclight and Houses of a Crystal Muse, and an adaptation of classic folk tales, Once

Upon a Time: Classic Folktales Reimagined. His work can be read at: johnbiscello.com

Mela Blust is a Pushcart Prize and three time Best of the Net nominee, and has appeared in The Bitter Oleander, Rust+Moth, The Nassau Review, The Sierra Nevada Review, Collective Unrest, and more. Her debut, *skeleton parade*, is available with Apep Publications. Her new full-length poetry collection, *they found a woman's body*, is available with Vegetarian Alcoholic Press. Mela is a contributing editor for Barren Magazine, and tweets at https://twitter.com/melablust.

Susi Bocks - writer/author/poet, has self-published two books - Feeling Human and Every Day I Pause - and is the Editor of The Short of It. You can find her work at IWriteHer.com or follow her on Facebook at MyHumanityInWrittenForm, where she invites you to read her thoughts and get to know her. Bocks' work has been published in the anthology SMITTEN: This Is What Love Looks Like: Poetry by Women for Women and in VitaBrevis, Spillwords, Literary Yard, as well as other literary magazines.

dani bowes is a twenty three year old retirement plan specialist by day, poet any other time. she enjoys practicing yoga and running, writing to her pen pals, and being a major coffee snob. you can connect with her via her poetry/personal instagram, @daniabowes

Ruth Bowley is the author of three books, both fiction and non-fiction. She also has a wide fan base with a very popular blog. When not writing, she spends her time with her two very active Bull Dogs and her partner of eighteen years. After an extremely difficult bout with Covid-19, her strength and health continue to improve, giving her a new appreciation for taking her time to enjoy life and to just be.

Marisela Brazfield was born and raised in urban Los Angeles and is a Gen X'er who chronicles and scrawls about the art form of living in the Angelino metropolitan environment; her offerings are inspired by the mental health crisis in the city. Marisela personally battles depression and anxiety but utilizes writing and art to self-regulate. WordPress address: https://wordslessspoken781842219.blog/
Twitter address: mb@tumblindice70

Cynthia L Bryant writes like she breathes, in and out. She served as Poet Laureate in the community of Pleasanton, CA 2005-2007 & 2011-2013. Her poetry has been published in numerous anthologies, website literary zines and literary magazines. Proudly she had three of her poems included in *We Will Not Be Silenced* 2018 Indie Blu(e) Publishing. Cynthia resides in Monterey, CA with Allen, Gracie Mae and Oscar Wilde. cynthialanebryant.com

D M Burton is a philosophy graduate from Bristol, UK. Primarily, Burton writes all kinds of poetry and creates a lot of blackout poetry. She has had poetry and prose featured in other anthologies, such as in *War Crimes Against The Uterus: Poems Of Resistance* by Wide Eyes Publishing (2019). Burton now tries to focus her efforts on politics and creates poetry in response to any significant political movements of the time, such as Black Lives Matter and issues surrounding the LGBTQ+ community.
DMBurton.co.uk   instagram.com/crazyaboutwords.db

Amie Campbell is an emerging poet based in Austin, TX. She enjoys spending her time with her children and rescue dog, and trying to keep her succulents alive. She has been published in the anthology, "SMITTEN: Women Who Love Women", antilang's "Pithy Politics" and the online literary review "Evocations". www.facebook.com/AmieCampbellAuthor

Jimmi Campkin: Writer and Photographer, a 16bit child with terminal nostalgia and red wine for blood. Read more at: www.jimmicampkin.com   www.jimmicampkinphotography.com

Jennifer Carr lives in Santa Fe, New Mexico with her partner and two children. She is an EMT, journalist, writer and poet. When she is not working at the local hospital or newspaper, she spends her time reading and writing poetry. Her poetry has been published in print and in many on-line publications. Her first poetry collection "Anything But Broken" was published in December 2019. Jennifer loves flying by her own wings and looks for any opportunity to soar to new heights. Don't forget to follow her on Twitter @PoetryHaiku13. Jennifer can also be found on Facebook as Jennifer Carr Munoz.

Teresa T. Chappell is a poet passionate about tethering the unseen onto the material. Her work can be found or is forthcoming from Coffin Bell Journal, Indie Blu(e) Publishing, Variant Literature, and Shiela-Na-Gig. Besides writing, her hobbies include: reading, eating, and swimming in the Long Island Sound.

John Cochrane Jr is a husband and father, computer programmer and poet. He is an ex-Mensan. He has played D&D off and on since 1977. He falls in love much too easily. He used to be young and brilliant, but is now merely old, somewhat smart, and perhaps a tiny bit wiser. He has a good heart, and tries to do the right thing. He is a lifelong Democrat.

Kai Coggin is a widely published poet and the author of three full-length poetry collections. She is a queer woman of color who thinks black lives matter, a teaching artist in poetry with the Arkansas Arts Council, and the host of the longest running consecutive weekly open mic series in the country— Wednesday Night Poetry. Recently named "Best Poet in Arkansas" by the Arkansas Times, her poetry has been nominated three times for The Pushcart Prize, as well as Bettering American Poetry 2015, and Best of the Net 2016 and 2018. She lives with her wife and their two adorable dogs in the valley of a small mountain in Hot Springs National Park, Arkansas.

Linda M. Crate's works have been published in numerous magazines and anthologies both online and in print. She is the author of six poetry chapbooks, the latest of which is: More Than Bone Music (Clare Songbirds Publishing House, March 2019). She's also the author of the novel Phoenix Tears (Czykmate Books, June 2018). Recently she has published two full-length poetry collections Vampire Daughter (Dark Gatekeeper Gaming, February 2020) and The Sweetest Blood (Cyberwit, February 2020).

Selene Crosier was born in Saint-Rémy-de-Provence and lives in America & France. Her day job involves lots of furry animals. Selene's heart belongs to the countryside, fresh air, kind people and ensuring equality. Selene's writing and artwork is published on many online poetry sites.

Writing is the song she continues to sing. Thoughts and images orchestrate with experiences in her mind. She takes her cues from people's smooth rough edges and lets her ink record their voices. To date, **Kimberly Cunningham** has three published books: Undefined, Sprinkles on Top, and Smooth Rough Edges as well as 30 plus published pieces. Kimberly has a BS in Education and MA in Curriculum and Instruction and teaches Special Ed preschoolers.

Candice Louisa Daquin edited SMITTEN This Is What Love Looks Like, Poetry By Women For Women, which won Indie Blu(e) a Finalist place in the National Indie Excellence Awards. She also worked as co-editor on We Will Not Be Silenced and splits her time between editing, writing and psychotherapy. www.thefeatheredsleep.com

Currently trudging through a first draft, **Katherine DeGilio** has three unpublished novels, a drawer full of poetry, and an intense Starbucks addiction. You can find her previous work in Third Wednesday, Scribble Lit, and Monsters Out of the Closet, among others. She loves connecting with her readers and encourages them to reach out to her through her website (Katherinedegilio.com) or on Twitter (@katiedegilio).

Liz DeGregorio is a writer and editor living in New York City. Her poems have been published in Indie Blu(e) Publishing's anthology "SMITTEN," Crack the Spine's anthology "Neighbors," Beyond Words Literary Magazine, Gravitas, The Tulane Review, Riva Collective's Chunk Lit and In Parentheses. Her flash fiction has appeared in *82 Review and Ruminate Magazine, and she's had fiction published in BUST Magazine.

Irma Do is a writer, runner, and raiser (of children not so much, plants or animals). She lives, out of her element, in the wilds of southeast Pennsylvania. Her writings are infused with the sweat and tears of an over-the-hill mother runner's race to make the world better before passing it down to her children. Her poetry and other writings can be found on her blog, iidorun.wordpress.com.

Jane Dougherty is the child of Irish emigrants, brought up in Yorkshire's Brontë country and emigrant in her own right to the southwest corner of France. She writes a lot, novels, short stories and poetry. Some of it has even been published. She blogs here incessantly https://janedougherty.wordpress.com/ and occasionally tweets here @MJDougherty33

Sarah Doughty is a Smashwords Most Downloaded Author with one poetry and multiple fiction books available, with more in the works. In addition, she has contributed to multiple current and upcoming books with standalone pieces or collaborations, such as Wild Is She, Poetica, Yellow, Crown Anthologies, and more. Her writing is featured in many publications across the web, including Brave And Reckless, Crossing Genres, and Sudden Denouement, along with its collective publications. As a survivor, she lives with complex PTSD and uses writing as a means to cope and heal, while connecting with people online through Instagram and WordPress. She lives in Indiana with her husband, young son, and a trio of misfit, therapeutic pets.

Matthew D. Eayre is a poet and writer from Monterey Bay California. Living a nomad life with his wife and children, he seeks truth, joy, and experience through poetic sight.

Melissa Fadul lives in New York with her wife and teaches advanced placement psychology and classical literature in a public high school in Queens, New York. She has been an educator for seventeen years. She has two loving and adorable pets: a Maltese dog named Linus and bunny named Roggie. Melissa is currently completing a poetry manuscript. For readings and appearances, you can contact Melissa at: melissafadul@gmail.com

Deirdre Fagan is a widow, wife, mother of two, and associate professor and coordinator of creative writing in the English, Literature, and World Languages Department at Ferris State University. Fagan is the author of a chapbook of poetry, Have Love, a forthcoming collection of short stories, The Grief Eater, and a reference book, Critical Companion to Robert Frost. Fagan writes poetry, fiction, nonfiction, and academic essays on poetry, memoir, and pedagogy. Meet her at deirdrefagan.com

Rachel Finch originally started using poetry as a way to accurately express herself after a number of traumatic experiences in her young life. She is the founder of Bruised But Not Broken which was started with the purpose to raise awareness of abuse and provide a place of comfort and support throughout the healing process. She believes that it was with the support of this community that she was able to recover from sexual abuse and move towards healing mind, body and soul. Rachel Finch is the author of 'A Sparrow Stirs Its Wings', 'Conversations With My Higher Self' and 'I am draped in Soul; it is a nakedness'. Her work has also been published in the anthologies 'We Will Not Be Silenced' and 'Smitten'.

Devereaux Frazier: Published poet and writer, contributor to Blood Into Ink, and Guest Barista for Go Dog Go Cafe. Regularly featured on SpillWords and nominated for the May Publication of the Month in 2017. Lately my poetry has shifted and focuses on the post-diagnosis life. The trauma of a confusing and abusive childhood created lines that are raw and heartfelt. Continuing in my road of recovery through introspection and a heavy dose of rhymes.
website: marylandpoetblog.wordpress.com
instagram: @d.frazier.writes

Nicholas Gagnier is the author of ten books, including the urban fantasy Shroud Saga, which includes the acclaimed novel Mercy Road, and the more recent Book of Death series of novels. He lives in Ottawa, Canada with his family.

Nadia Garofalo is an artist/musician/poet currently living in Chicago. She freelances on TV and film crews. She is a founding member of the post-punk band Ganser. She writes lyrics collaboratively in the music produced by Ganser. You can find Ganser's music at www.ganser.bandcamp.com. Her poetry has been published by Whisper and the Roar as well as Indie Blu(e) Publishing in the book Smitten: This is What Love Looks Like. Read her at https://medium.com/@nadiagarofalo

Anthony Glenn is a writer of prose, fiction, poetry, and non-fiction sociological diatribes. He has written on his website since 2014. Rarely does he miss his self-enforced publication schedule of Monday-Wednesday-Friday. If pressed, he will say his style could be called incendiary, sensual, and minimalist. However, he prefers his readers to be the judge.
www.pelgris.com

F.I. Goldhaber's words capture people, places, and politics with a photographer's eye and a poet's soul. As a reporter, editor, and business writer, they produced news stories, features, editorials, and reviews for newspapers, corporations, governments, and non-profits in five states. Now paper, electronic, and audio magazines, books, newspapers, calendars, broadsides, and street signs display their poetry, fiction, and essays. More than 160 of their poems appear in almost 70 publications, including four collections. http://www.goldhaber.net/

Maria Gray is a 20-year-old poet from Portland, Oregon. Her work can be found in Snaggletooth Magazine and Counterclock Journal and has been nominated for Best of the Net. She is the recipient of awards from Bates College, Portland State University, Oregon Poetry Association, National Federation of State Poetry Societies, and others, as well as an alum of the Adroit Journal Summer Mentorship Program and Counterclock Journal's Counterclock Arts Collective, where she spent a month as a writing fellow.

Ali Grimshaw contributes to the world as an educator, life coach, and a poet. She is passionate about leading shared writing experiences so others may experience the power of their own voices. Her poems have been published in anthologies and journals including, Vita Brevis, Right Hand Pointing and Ghost City Review. You can find her writing circle offerings and her poetry at flashlightbatteries.blog.

Velma Hamilton lives in Northern California where she loves the inspiration of the beautiful landscape available at her fingertips. Her aspirations include composing a short book of her written works. She is currently on a path of gaining inner peace and strength as the current pandemic has affected her livelihood. Poetry is a most effective outlet. Velma is positive we will all be alright and looks forward to the future.

Kim Harvey is a Pushcart Prize and Best of the Net nominee and an Associate Editor at Palette Poetry. You can find her work in Barren Magazine, Black Bough Poetry, Kissing Dynamite, Poets Reading the News, Radar, Rattle, SWWIM, The Shore, trampset, and other journals. Her poems also appear in the following anthologies: Smitten: This is What Love Looks Like, Undeniable: Writers Respond to Climate Change, and Written Here: The Community of Writers Poetry Review 2017. She is the 1st Prize winner of the Comstock Review's 2019 Muriel Craft Bailey Memorial Award and the 3rd Prize winner of the 2019 Barren Press Poetry Contest. She has two microchaps available from Kissing Dynamite Press and Ghost City Press. Twitter: @kimharveypoet
Instagram: @luna_jack   Blog: www.kimharvey.net

Hoda is a New Orleans based, East African writer who jots down love notes from the Universe and has the pleasure of calling them poetry. An educator and maker, Hoda writes to live, to breathe and find heaven.

Hokis is an American poet of Armenian descent. She is Senior Editor of Headline Poetry & Press and regular contributor to Reclamation Magazine. Her upcoming collection "On Becoming" is a poetic memoir detailing her personal rise from political trauma. Creative nonfiction as foreshadowing preface, and other published works, are found on hokis.blog.

In the pre-COVID world, **Kelsey Hontz** was a drag performer, pole dance enthusiast, and sometimes writer. Now she is a zoom moderator, protest enthusiast, and sometimes writer. She is grateful for Indie Blu(e)'s continued support; her writing can also be found in 2019's anthology SMITTEN: This Is What Love Looks Like.

Tia M. Hudson lives in Bremerton, Washington, where she teaches English at Olympic College. In March of 2019, she was appointed Poet Laureate of Bremerton. Her poems have been published in Wend Poetry Journal, The Stillwater Review, Signals, and the anthology Smitten: This is What Love Looks Like. Poetry By Women for Women. She has also had five poems presented in 2015 and 2016's Ars Poetica, – a yearly collaboration between poets and visual artists in Kitsap County, and two ekphrastic poems published on the website of the Museum of Northwest Art in LaConner.

Maria Gianna Iannucci is a science educator, poet, and mother. She has a background in neuroscience and education and currently teaches at the Bullis School in Potomac, MD and The University of Notre Dame in Indiana. Maria Gianna is the co-founder of Capitalwise Press and owner of Crosstree Press, two independent publishing companies. She published *Luminarium*, a collection of written and spoken word poetry in 2019. Maria currently lives in Maryland.

Rachael Z. Ikins is a 2016/18 Pushcart, 2013/18 CNY Book Award, 2018 Independent Book Award winner, & 2019 Vinnie Ream & Faulkner poetry finalist. She is author/illustrator of 9 books in multiple genres. Born in the Fingerlakes she lives by a river with her dogs, cats, salt water fish, a garden that feeds her through winter and riotous houseplants with a room of their own. Dragons fly by.

Sarah Ito. I am a published novelist, essayist, poet and actor. I am an Army veteran and actively involved in Human Rights issues worldwide.

Jessica Jacobs is the author of *Take Me with You, Wherever You're Going* (Four Way Books), a memoir-in-poems of early marriage, winner of the Goldie Award in Poetry and one of *Library Journal*'s best poetry books of the year. Her debut collection, *Pelvis with Distance* (White Pine Press), a biography-in-poems of Georgia O'Keeffe, won the New Mexico Book Award in Poetry and was a finalist for the Lambda Literary Award. An avid long-distance runner, Jessica has worked as a rock-climbing instructor, bartender, and professor, and now serves as the Chapbook Editor of *Beloit Poetry Journal*. She lives in Asheville, North Carolina, with her wife, poet Nickole Brown, with whom she co-authored *Write It! 100 Poetry Prompts to Inspire* (Spruce Books/PenguinRandom House)

Ashley Jane is an indie author from Alabama. She is a former Substance Abuse Counselor with research published in Crime and Delinquency magazine. She is the co-founder of FallsPoetry prompts. She also co-runs DarkLines and DrugVerse prompts on Twitter, and Her Heart Poetry on Instagram. She has three books of poetry out: Love, Lies and Lullabies, The Mums are Filled with Melancholy and All Darkness and Dahlias. She enjoys books, music, travel, and helping other authors pursue their dreams of publishing. Links: www.instagram.com/breathwords
Blog: www.breathwords.com www.facebook.com/breathwords
www.twitter.com/breathwords

Sun Hesper Jansen is a writer of queer-normative romantic high fantasy, magical realism, and poetry who divides her time between south-central Wisconsin and northern New Mexico. She is the author of the blog 'Away from the Machine' (awayfromthemachine.wordpress.com) where she writes on/as literary therapy for multiple sclerosis.

Carol H. Jewell is a musician, teacher, librarian, and poet, living in Upstate New York. Nearing the end of her career as a librarian, Carol is involved in many writing projects, which bring both challenges and satisfaction. A chapbook of her poems has been published, she has work included in two anthologies, is currently editing an anthology of pantoums, occasionally gives a workshop on poetry writing for healing, and teaches a college lecture on pantoums.

Annette Kalandros, a retired teacher, residing in Houston, TX with two French Bulldogs, writes to make sense of things— life, the world, the inner workings of her own mind and soul. In addition, she had been active in the LGBTQ community since she was four years old and marched her Ken doll with all his little Ken accoutrements to the big metal trash can in the yard. Her two Barbie dolls lived happily ever after. You can read more of her writing at https://aikalandros.com/

Destiny Killian is a freelance editor and aspiring poet. She is currently a senior English and Liberal Arts double major at Shorter University. Following graduation, she hopes to work as an editor for a publishing company. When she's not reading or writing, she enjoys talking with her friends and spending time with her two cats.

Crystal Kinistino is a poet and lover of the written word. She has been previously published in Decanto Poetry Magazine and the anthology; We Will Not Be Silenced. She blogs at https://thoughtslikecages.wordpress.com/. She is inspired by such strong feminist writers as Virginia Woolf, Sylvia Plath and Anne Sexton. She draws her inspiration from nature and life. She is a proud lesbian, radical feminist and half-blood Cree woman residing in the treaty #1 territory of Canada.

Erik Klingenberg: I am an English language poet, photographer, musician and former archaeologist who has lived and worked in Europe for 40 years. Educated in the United States with a B.A. in English Literature and Creative Writing, I try to present a labyrinth of canvases painted with language and mazes of words sculpted with sound. I write my pieces to be read aloud and combine them with my own photos. My blog is: Nightpoetry (nitepoetry.wordpress.com).

Detroit born and raised, **Mandy Kocsis** is a poet lost in Indiana, where she cares for her mother (the strongest woman she's ever known), and her amazing son. She is the author "Soul Survivor", a poetic autobiography, and you can find more of her work at Mandy's Land on Facebook.

Eleanór Knight is a 19-year-old Americana singer-songwriter, multi-instrumentalist and producer from North Devon, England. Her songs and poetry bring forth musings and tales of love, longing and loss.

Rachel Kobin, writer, photographer, and editor, founded The Philadelphia Writers' Workshop to provide a structured and supportive forum where writers can express themselves freely, experiment, and hone their craft. When her eye doctor

suggested she look away from her computer regularly to relieve eye strain, she began taking pictures of the view out her window and writing about what she sees and feels.
Instagram: @Kobichrome and @philadelphiawritersworkshop; Facebook: /WritewithRachel; Linkedin: /rachel-m-kobin/ Twitter: @RachelKobin

Kendall Krantz is a writer and undergrad at Brown University. She is pursuing a B.A. in Urban Studies. Her work can be found in publications such as McSweeney's, Vice Motherboard, and the Kurt Vonnegut Literary Magazine, among others.

Aakriti Kuntal is a poet and writer from Gurugram, India. Her work has been featured in various literary magazines. She was awarded the Reuel International Prize 2017 for poetry and was a finalist for the RL Poetry Award 2018. Her poem Lilith was nominated for the Best of the Net 2018-19 by the Pangolin Review.

A. Lawler is a university student who enjoys writing poetry (as many university students do).

John W. Leys is an indie poet living in Oregon with his chihuahua, Cosmo. He has had poetry published in Nicholas Gagnier's *All the Lonely People* and David L. O'Nan's tribute to Leonard Cohen, *Avalanches in Poetry*. His first poetry collection, *The Darkness of His Dreams*, was published in 2019. Twitter: @eliyahu5733.
Blog: http://DarknessOfHisDreams.wordpress.com
Facebook: facebook.com/darknessofhisdreams/

Aviva Lilith is a poet and artist currently living in Manchester, New Hampshire. Twitter: aviva_lilith Instagram: aviva_lilith Email: avivalilith@gmail.com

A North Carolina writer, **Tremaine L. Loadholt** has been published in literary journals, anthologies, and magazines, and published three poetry books: Pinwheels and Hula Hoops, Dusting for Fingerprints, and A New Kind of Down. She's editor and creative director for Quintessence: A Literary Magazine of Featured Medium Writers. Her artistic expressions are at A Cornered Gurl, Medium, and Twitter.

emje mccarty inks with bamboo pens & brushes. she likes to experiment with writing & inking graphic novels. emje journals almost daily & publishes her art journal pages over on quixoticmama.com. she has published a book of neurotic comics & has a collection of self-portraits titled "the invisible exhibitionist" which will be showing soon in the driftless area of wisconsin where she lives & raises a horde of anarchists.

Andrew McDowell has been writing since he was a child. He has published poetry, fiction, and creative nonfiction. His novel *Mystical Greenwood* was a finalist in the 2019 American Fiction Awards for Fantasy: Epic/High Fantasy. Andrew is a member of the Maryland Writers' Association. Visit his website and blog at andrewmcdowellauthor.com to learn more about him and his work.

Sean Heather K. McGraw, Ph.D. is an adjunct lecturer of history and philosophy at several colleges. She has also worked as a librarian and a National Park Historic Site guide. In her spare time, she studies various languages, plays several musical instruments, primarily the harp and ukulele, writes poetry and works unendingly at the novel she hopes to one day publish. Contact her at drseanheathermcgraw@gmail.com.

Dawn D. McKenzie grew up in Europe but lived in the USA for a decade, where she still keeps many friends from all social, religious and political backgrounds, which gives her a unique insight into American society. She shares her time between her family, her job and writing. She is currently writing the first book in what will be a trilogy and is excited to see how it all comes out.

Tamara J. Madison is an author, poet, editor, and instructor. Her critical and creative works have been recorded, produced, and published in various journals, magazines, exhibits, podcasts, and anthologies. Her most recent poetry collection Threed, This Road Not Damascus was published by Trio House Press (May 2019).

Devika Mathur resides in India and is a published poet, writer. Her works have been published or are upcoming in Madras Courier, Modern Literature, Two Drops Of Ink, Dying Dahlia Review, Pif Magazine, Spillwords, Duane's Poetree, Piker Press, Mojave heart review, Whisper and the Roar amongst various others. She is the founder of the surreal poetry website "Olive skins." & writes for She recently published a poetry collection, *Crimson Skins*.
Blog: https://myvaliantsoulsblog.wordpress.com/.
Instagram @my.valiant.soul

Lindz McLeod's short stories have been published by the Scotsman newspaper, the Scottish Book Trust, the Dundee Victoria & Albert Museum, and more. Her poetry has been published by Allegory Ridge, Prismatica, and more. Lindz is the competition secretary of the Edinburgh Writer's Club, and her writing can be found at www.lindzmcleod.co.uk

Johann Morton: I am the founder of Morton Labs. Being black, "Fitting The Description" during police stops and dirty looks from passers-by as though I were a mugger (or worse) is "normal". It was worse in the past, before "Political Correctness" happened. But in recent years, some have taken Brexit and Trump's election as a legitimisation of racism and bigotry. The pandemic has only exacerbated the situation; a failing economy, increasing domestic abuse, mass unemployment. These are dark times.

I am **Nayana Nair**, an engineer and a technical writer who moonlights as an amateur poet on my personal blog (itrainsinmyheart.wordpress.com). Writing for me is a process of self-realization and an effort to understand what is ever elusive.

Allie Nelson is a Science Editor by day and writer by night. Her works have appeared in Sudden Denouement, FunDead Publications, Apex Magazine, Eternal Haunted Summer, the Showbear Family Circus, Frontiers in Health Communication, POWER Magazine, Renewable Energy World, and she previously won the Goronwy Owen Poetry Prize, judged by acclaimed poet Kazim Ali.

Lesléa Newman has created 75 books for readers of all ages including the poetry collections, Still Life with Buddy, October Mourning: A Song for Matthew Shepard (novel-in-verse), I Carry My Mother, and I Wish My Father. Her literary awards include poetry fellowships from the National Endowment for the Arts and the Massachusetts Artists Foundation. A past poet laureate of Northampton, Massachusetts, she currently teaches at Spalding University's School of Creative and Professional Writing.

Jesica Nodarse is a Cuban-born immigrant living in Florida, with her husband and children. A powerful writer and poet, an intense and driven woman, Jesica offers her unique perspective in today's world and empowers her friends and colleagues with passion and grace. Jesica can be found on Facebook at facebook.com/heathenwordsmith and on Instagram at https://www.instagram.com/j.nodarse/

Robert Okaji is a displaced Texan living in Indiana. The author of five chapbooks, his work has appeared or is forthcoming in Taos Journal of International Poetry & Art, Atlanta Review, North Dakota Quarterly, Glass: A Journal of Poetry, and elsewhere.

Sammie Payne has been an active poet for the last 18 years covering a number of different subjects but focusing on mental health. Sammie is also a keen photographer specializing in wildlife and nature.

Dustin Pickering is founding editor of Harbinger Asylum and co-owner of Transcendent Zero Press. He is a Pushcart nominee and former contributor to Huffington Post. He placed as finalist in Adelaide Literary Journal's short fiction contest in 2018. He is also an essayist, painter, and philosopher. He lives alone in Houston, Texas.

Rob Plath is a writer from New York. He was once tutored by Allen Ginsberg for two years from 1995-1997. He has published 22 books and a ton of poems in the small presses over the last 26 years. He lives with his cat and tries his best to stay out of trouble.

S.A. Quinox is a young Belgian and modern poet that writes for the aching, the yearning and the mad wanderers among us. She loves to write about the dark night of the soul, the parts that we so desperately try to keep hidden. Quinox can be found on social media through Facebook and Instagram.

Christine E. Ray lives outside of Philadelphia, Pennsylvania. A former Managing Editor of Sudden Denouement Publications, she founded Indie Blu(e) Publishing with Kindra M. Austin in September 2018. Ray is author of *Composition of a Woman* and *The Myths of Girlhood*. Her writing is also featured in *SMITTEN This Is What Love Looks Like*, *We Will Not Be Silent*, *Anthology Volume I: Writings from the Sudden Denouement Literary Collective, Swear to Me*, and *All the Lonely People*. Read more of her work at https://braveandrecklessblog.com/.

Kristiana Reed is a writer and an English teacher living in the UK. She is the creator of My Screaming Twenties and sole Editor of Free Verse Revolution on WordPress. Reed has released two poetry collections: Between the Trees and Flowers on the Wall. Both collections are available on Amazon. You can follow her on Instagram, @kristianamst, and Facebook, @myscreamingtwenties.

Hanlie Robbertse is a creative writer, reader and thinker. She is passionate about being her best self and she brings this passion into her work too. She tries to lead by example and believe firmly that our actions, not just our words, define who we really are. You can find her writing at:
Facebook: https://www.facebook.com/IamHanlie/

Instagram: hanlie.robbertse

Dr. Sneha Rooh is a palliative physician and founder of Orikalankini, an organization that is changing narratives around Menstruation and sexuality in India through art theatre and dialogue. She loves to travel and write.

Rachel W. Roth is a graduate of the University of South Florida in St. Petersburg with a bachelor's degree in English and a Certificate in Creative Writing. Her poetry and short fiction has been featured in multiple literary journals and anthologies.

My name is **Charu Sharma** and I am 26 years old, I am from India. I have been writing poetry since 2016. Since then my writing style has been exposed to a lot of changes owing to my exploration with both different writers and genres in both prose and poems. I only mean to express the horrors, the lucid moments of truth, the gut wrenching pain and at times a wee bit of peace.

My name is Angie Waters. I am a writer/artist who uses the alias **A. Shea**. My work often reflects my own healing process as a trauma survivor as well as my fight to maintain my mental health and live well with chronic illness. You can find me on Facebook at www.facebook.com/a.sheawriter and Instagram @a.sheawriter

As one half of the Unbolt Me creative duo, **Tony Single** has co-authored two poetry anthologies ('One Pulse: Cradle 2 Grave' and 'Love Death Hell') and co-produced three webcomics ('Crumble Cult', 'Marth & Bramwell' and

'Trottersville'). He also plays videogames and writes countless angsty poems in his free time, as is his wont. www.unbolt.me

Izabell Jöraas Skoogh has studied creative writing as an international student-athlete at Saint Leo University in Tampa, FL, for a couple of years. Her piece "Under the Surface" was published in the Sandhill Review Magazine in 2017, and three pieces published in the anthology Smitten This Is What Love Looks Like, Poetry by Women for Women in 2019.

Jamie L. Smith received her MFA in creative writing from Hunter College. Her work appears or is forthcoming from the Bellevue Literary Review, Not-Very-Quiet, Peculiar, Pigeon Pages, San Antonio Review, Tusculum Review, and the Indie Blu(e) anthology Smitten: Poetry by Women for Women. She lives in Salt Lake City, where she is a PhD candidate in English at the University of Utah.

Merril D. Smith is a historian and poet. She has written and edited several books on history, gender, and sexuality. Her poetry and short fiction have appeared recently in Black Bough Poetry, Twist in Time, Nightingale and Sparrow, and Wellington Street Review. Web site: merrildsmith.com.
Twitter: @merril_mds   Instagram: mdsmithnj

Megha Sood is an Assistant Poetry Editor at MookyChick(UK). Over 450+ works in journals including FIVE:2: ONE, Dime Show Review, Kissing Dynamite, Poetry Society of New York, etc.Three-time State-level Winner NJ Poetry Contest 2018/2019/2020, National level Winner Spring Robinson Prize, Finalist Pangolin Poetry Prize 2019, Adelaide Literary Award 2019. Currently co-editing anthologies ("The Medusa Project", MookyChick), and ("The Kali Project", Indie Blu(e) Publishing).

Blogs at https://meghasworldsite.wordpress.com/
Tweets at @meghasood16

L. Stevens is an intj who loves learning about everything and filing it all away for later. She writes short stories and poetry about the moon, darkness, and anything else lurking in the deep abyss of her imagination. Her work has been featured by Pack Poetry, Free Verse Revolution, and Heretics, Lovers, and Madmen. More of her work can be seen at everyday-strange.com and on Instagram @everydaystrangeblog

Eric Syrdal is an independent poet/author. He's an avid gamer and Sci-Fi enthusiast. He enjoys reading science fiction and fantasy literature. In 2018, he published his first novel, a tale written in epic verse, with Indie Blu(e) Publishing entitled "Pantheon". He is from New Orleans, Louisiana, where he lives with his wife and two children.

Rachel Tijou: Mother of five, amateur photographer, deep thinker, shy singer, lifelong writer of words in my mind, which are patiently awaiting pen and paper.

With a B.A. and M.A. in British and American literature, **Carla Toney**'s poetry anthology, *After the Burning*, was published by Beothuk Books in 2001. Her historical research, *No Man's Land: "Multitribal Indians" in the United States* has been described as "*a tour de force* of detailed research and scholarship" (New Century Press, 2019). It focuses on "multitribal Indians" including the Cherokee Chickamaugans and their allies, Shawnees, Creeks, British loyalists, and former slaves. Contact: carla46@gmx.co.uk

My name is **Char Trolinder** and I am a 36 year old proud lesbian woman that loves the simple life. I work 5+ days a week at my job, when I do have down time I love to spend it with my fur babies, Tink and Pete, and my family. I love to read because books are my escape from the world. I started writing as a form of therapy for my depression and anxiety. Now it has kind of become my voice to the world. When I was asked to participate in this I was speechless because I've never really seen my writing as earth moving. I hope and wish for all peace, love, and the ability to proudly be who we are as individuals.

Erin Van Vuren is an LGBTQ Southern California native in love with her fiancé, animals, and writing. She believes wholeheartedly in the power of imagination and kindness. She will forever push for all young women and LGBTQ youth to chase and capture their dreams, and to know they are never alone.

Philip Vernon, MA: Years of living life as a type of existential ethnic power-broker — the quintessential mediator — can be traced back to when my Norwegian mother and creole Father (French, Black, Native American) met on campus, in Madison. From my earliest recollection I remember being taught to defy simplistic cartoon labels and anti-intellectual expectations created by the weak of intellect. Writing The Tan Millennium, a screenplay adaptation of the scholarly research that formed the basis of my Masters thesis, I felt I reached my calling,and in it, a voice for many others. Media outlets published it, as the work became one of the first written by a multi-ethnic person for the there-to-fore yet numerical significant and growing bi and multi-ethnic US population.
Read more at https://blowbackmultimedia.wordpress.com

Petru J Viljoen: On a personal level, lockdown during Covid-19 is an old normal. Business as usual. However, the global environment has been shaken so badly, circumstances change and did change so quickly, the momentum of the waves of Covid requires one to stay flexible, informed and yes, somewhat angry. Participating in local and global conversation is vital.

Marvlyn C. Vincent was born and raised in the Caribbean. She migrated to the United States more than a decade ago, not just in search of a better life, but also to literally save her life. As a child Marvlyn started writing poetry as an escape from the horrors of her reality, but also as an outlet for her pain. This was her way of sharing the things that she could not speak about. Today she still writes about her past experiences, however, she's also developed her writing to include the resolution that has gotten her through the hard times.

Philip A. Wardlow's writings run to all the various forms, from poetry, to short stories, to essays, to a self-published dark urban fantasy novella. He dabbles in the sexy, the darkness of the soul, the humorous, the profound, and beautifully sentimental reflective sides of life. He has written to his Blog for over eight years at www.philipwardlow.com entitled, "Ain't no Rest for the Wicked" to hone his writing and expand his following.

Milly Webster is a 22-year-old poet and student. She has just finished her undergraduate dissertation, a collection of poetry centred around bisexuality and bi-erasure. She is Assistant Managing Editor at The Lincoln Review. In October she will be beginning her Master's degree in Creative Writing at The

University of Lincoln. Twitter: @MillyLouise2 Instagram: @milly.webster

Marcia J. Weber dreamt of becoming a writer as a child. That dream was tabled as she pursued a career, family life and motherhood. In the midst of a life changing squall, writing became her life raft. She has been published in The Poetic Bond VII and VIII, Orion Magazine, Writings from Sudden Denouement Literary Collective, We Will Not Be Silenced, and electronically on Spillwords. She writes as Aurora Phoenix at Insights from "Inside".

Carrie L. Weis is the Museum and Gallery Director at Ferris State University overseeing the Art Gallery, University Collections, and the Card/Riley Conservation and Wildlife Education Center. She holds a Master of Fine Arts in Painting from Kendall College of Art & Design, and a B.I.S. degree with a major in Studio Fine Art and a minor in Art History from Ferris State University Artistically, Weis has been painting for over 30 years and continues an active studio practice. She participates in solo and group exhibitions and art residencies. The most current being at the Golden Apple Artist Residency in Harrington Maine during the summer of 2019. Her current series titled Nature Divine expresses the spiritual in nature as she immerses herself in journeys to wild and natural places throughout the United States. www.weiscreative.org

Lola White: I'm a poet/ photographer, in Nashville, TN. When I regularly submit work, I regularly publish it, but in recent years, I've become sloth-like regarding submission, and thus suffer a paucity of publication. Some years ago, at seventy, for fear that in taking the traditional route to publishing, I would die before achieving publication, I self-published a poetry collection titled

"The Seed at Center", and was invited to read from it at the Southern Festival of Books.

Melita White is an Australian poet and writer of essays and creative nonfiction. Her writing is feminist and confessional in style and focuses on topics such as MeToo and familial and intimate partner abuse. She hopes to spread awareness of these topics through her writing and help other survivors feel that they are not alone in their experiences of abuse. Visit her blog Feminist Confessional to read more of her work: http://feministconfessional.wordpress.com

Karissa Whitson. A college student who lives with five pets, four with four legs, one with two, and loves them all equally. School will always come first, but writing is a love that cannot be pushed aside.

Sally Zakariya's poetry has appeared in some 75 print and online journals and been nominated for the Pushcart Prize and Best of the Net. Her most recent publication is *Muslim Wife* (Blue Lyra Press, 2019). She is also the author of *The Unknowable Mystery of Other People, Personal Astronomy, When You Escape, Insectomania,* and *Arithmetic and other verses,* as well as the editor of a poetry anthology, Joys of the Table. Zakariya blogs at www.butdoesitrhyme.com.